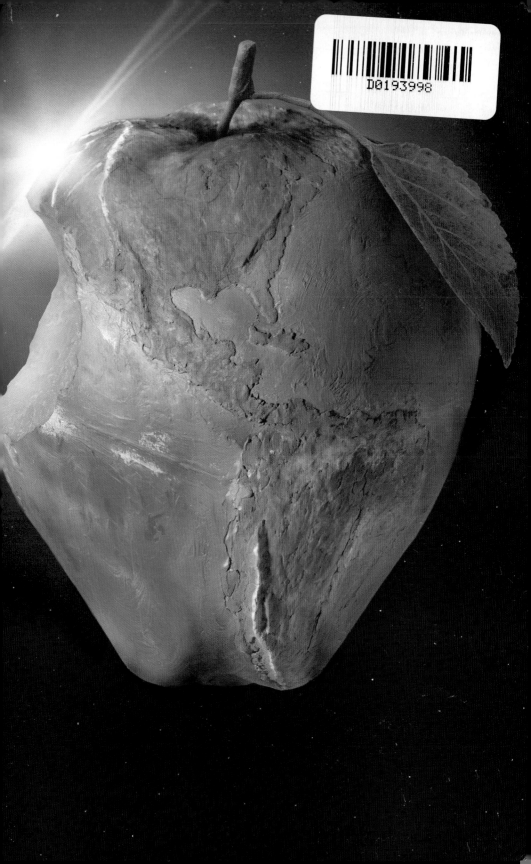

THE LIE

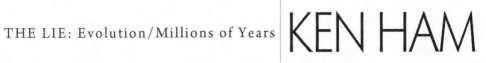

THE LIE: Evolution/Millions of Years | KEN HAM

ANNIVERSARY EDITION

25

YEARS

REVISED & EXPANDED

LiE

THE LIE:
Evolution/Millions of Years

KEN HAM

Master
Books®

First printing: July 1987
Thirty-second printing: March 2011
Revised edition: September 2012
Revised edition, 2nd printing: November 2012

Enter The Lie Photo Contest offering 25 weeks of prizes and a BIG Grand Prize — see page 240

Master Books®, P.O. Box 726, Green Forest, AR 72638
Master Books® is a division of the New Leaf Publishing Group, Inc.

ISBN: 978-0-89051-686-7 (paperback)
ISBN: 978-0-89051-716-1 (casebound)
ISBN: 978-1-61458-272-4 (ebook)
Library of Congress Number: 00-108776

Front cover photo: Rockafellow Photography, Springfield, MO

Cover: Diana Bogardus

Interior illustrations: Dan Lietha, Steve Cardno, Daniel Lewis, and Jon Seest

Unless otherwise noted, Scripture verses are from the New King James Version of the Holy Bible.

Please consider requesting that a copy of this volume be purchased by your local library system.

Printed in the United States of America

Please visit our website for other great titles:
www.masterbooks.net

For information regarding author interviews,
please contact the publicity department at (870) 438-5288.

Master Books®
A Division of New Leaf Publishing Group
www.masterbooks.net

DEDICATION

This updated version is still dedicated to the same three special people without whom this publication would not have been possible.

To my mother and father for their stand on the Scriptures, their insistence on purity of doctrine, and their uncompromising acceptance of God's Word and the principles therein, which they applied to every area of life. Their example equipped me so a higher authority (the Lord) could call me into full-time service for Him. I thank God for this Christian training and my parents' stand on the infallible Word of God. As of this writing, my mother still lives in Australia, but my father has passed on to glory. In the Creation Museum (opened in 2007) there is an exhibit with my father's Bible and a small Noah's Ark model he built me, together with video and photographs of my father and mother. This exhibit stands as a testimony to godly parents and a challenge to others concerning what kind of legacy they are leaving in their children.

To my dear wife, Mally, who has truly been one with me in all aspects of our married life (in our 38th year of marriage as of the updating of this book) and in our participation in creation ministry. Her sincere Christian dedication and devotion in regard to my involvement in this vital ministry can be summed up by the words of Ruth, in Ruth 1:16, "For wherever you go, I will go; And wherever you lodge, I will lodge." A special chapter entitled "A Girl Called Ruth," in the book my brother Stephen and I authored called *Raising Godly Children in an Ungodly World*, explains more about this special Ruth testimony. Mally's special, God-given abilities and her love for children have been a real blessing to our five dear children (and at the writing of this dedication, our ten grandchildren — one of whom is still in the womb) and have enabled me to widely proclaim the message of the authority of Scripture and the gospel to millions of people in various parts of the world through the creation ministry now known as Answers in Genesis. Truly, the Creation Museum (which has seen over a million visitors since opening) is a legacy of godly parents and a godly, devoted wife.

ACKNOWLEDGMENTS

This book is now a culmination of over 30 years of experience in the creation/biblical authority ministry that began in our house in Australia and has now spread around the world — one of the climaxes being the opening of the Creation Museum in the Greater Cincinnati area (USA) in 2007.

It would be impossible to recall all those who have helped and influenced me along the way.

When we inaugurated the Creation Science Foundation ministry in Australia in the late '70s, we certainly did not realize the far-reaching effects this ministry would have in different parts of the world.

The original manuscript of *The Lie* was typed by Carol Van Luyn. Little did she know that this work would be a bestseller in the creation ministry for 25 years before it needed revising and updating. I would like to acknowledge my good friend and artist Steve Cardno, who, with tireless expenditure of his God-given talents, produced the original illustrations used in the first publication of this book. Other artists have now built on the work that Steve accomplished and have updated the illustrations. The "castle diagrams" Steve originally drew, even though now modified, still remain to this day the classic illustrations that portray the message of the Answers in Genesis ministry. The name of Dr. Gary Parker appears on occasion throughout this book. Dr. Parker is a well-known creationist speaker and author who became an integral part of the initial outreach of Answers in Genesis when it was founded in 1994. I have had the privilege of appearing with him on various platforms in Australia and the United States. Many experiences we shared together before the manuscript was first written have contributed to parts of this book.

I would like to thank Dan Lietha, AiG's long-time cartoonist and illustrator, for the many hours he devoted to preparing the illustrations for this new edition. I would also like to thank Steve Golden, my research assistant, for the considerable time he spent in research for this updated manuscript, and also in its editing.

Last, I would like to sincerely thank the late Dr. Henry Morris, who is considered the father of the modern creation movement. He, along with Dr. John Whitcomb, authored the classic *The Genesis Flood*, which was the first major biblical creationist book that had a great influence on my thinking. Also, Dr. Morris's book *The Genesis Record* had a profound influence on my understanding of the relevance of the book of Genesis. It was this book that inspired my first sermon on "The Relevance of Genesis," which really began my main teaching ministry in the creation movement. To all my friends and colleagues who have been towers of strength to me over the past many years — thank you.

CONTENTS

There is a war in society — Christianity versus humanism. Too few Christians realize that the essence of the conflict lies firmly at the foundational level — God's Word versus man's word. Because it is beneficial in waging successful warfare to first identify the field, this chapter establishes the true nature of the battlefield.

The media and the public education system tell us that creation cannot be taught in schools because it is religion, while evolution is science. It is easy to grasp the basic tenets of science and quickly come to the conclusion that evolution is really a religion.

Creation and evolution are equally scientific and religious. The controversy is not religion versus science but the authority of God's Word versus man's fallible words. Will we trust the Word of the One who was there or the word of fallible man?

The reason people do not want to accept creation is that it means there is a Creator who sets the rules. Thus, no person can write his own rules.

Eliminate Genesis, and the structure of Christianity will begin to collapse. Opinion-oriented (evolution/millions of years-based) philosophy, rather than thinking rooted in the authority of God's Word, is destroying society.

Many Christians fail to realize that the events of Genesis are literal, are historical (particularly Genesis 1–11), and are foundational to all Christian doctrine. All biblical doctrines of theology, directly or indirectly, ultimately have their basis in the Book of Genesis. Therefore, a believing understanding of the Book of Genesis is a prerequisite to an understanding of God and His meaning to man. If Genesis is only myth or allegory, then Christian doctrines have no foundation.

Many Christians have added evolution/millions of years to the Bible, resulting in a position that accepts God as Creator but sheds doubt on the trustworthiness of Genesis. The position is destructive to Christianity for many reasons.

There is an easy-to-understand reason why death and suffering exist in a world created by a God of love. Evolutionary ideas, which teach death and struggle over millions of years, destroy the foundation of the message of the Cross.

The growing acceptance of atheistic evolution and therefore man's word as the starting point has resulted in many rejecting God as Creator. Over the years, many have used evolution to justify abortion, communism, Nazism, drug abuse, homosexual practices, and worse. Increase in the popularity of evolution has gone hand in hand with the increase in popularity of these social issues. While evolution is not to blame for the social ills of society, it has become the justification for lending respectability to such social attitudes. The ultimate cause of these problems is the rejection of God's Word as the starting point and thus the rejection of God as Creator.

Creation evangelism may be a new term to many, but it is a biblical method. Paul used it with great success. Creation evangelism is a tool the church needs to use to restore the right foundation in order to present the whole gospel message. Evolution/millions of years is one of the biggest barriers to today's people being receptive to the gospel of Jesus Christ. Creation evangelism is a powerful method that removes these barriers and opens people's hearts and minds to the gospel.

A plea to pastors and other religious leaders to see the importance of the creation/evolution issue. It is not a side issue. Many religious leaders do not realize that the true nature of the evolution/ millions of years controversy is an attack on biblical authority because they have been hoodwinked into thinking that what they have been led to believe is true science. The church is suffering greatly because many have compromised with evolutionary ideas.

A message and warning from 2 Peter 3 concerning the rejection in the last days of the belief in God as Creator. This should be a real warning to everyone of the importance of origins. The prophecy in 2 Peter 3 concerning the last days is being fulfilled before our very eyes.

Appendixes

The material in the appendixes is meant to provide detailed answers to the questions people have concerning how the message of creation evangelism has changed over the years.

FOREWORD

THIS BOOK WAS WRITTEN in 1986 and first published in 1987. In 2012, I set out to revise and update this work, which still represents the essence of the message the Lord has called me to proclaim to the church and world. I have received more testimonies concerning changed lives from this book than any other I have written. Even though the basic message has not changed in the 25 years since I wrote this work, that same message has matured considerably, and I believe this updated version to be many times more powerful than the original.

The late Luther D. Sunderland wrote the original foreword. Since the basic message of the book has remained the same, I want this original foreword to remain also, as a tribute to the creation ministry of Luther Sunderland.

Ken Ham

****

Perhaps you have not been notably successful in winning friends and acquaintances to the life-changing belief in God and His Son, Jesus Christ. You might have wondered why the Christian church in general seems to be losing ground in its battle with the evils of the secular world. Not only does this book identify the reason for such problems, but it also offers an effective solution. When you read Ken Ham's logical analysis of the situation and the straightforward way in which he proposes to correct it, you will likely say, "Why didn't I think of that?"

At an ever-accelerating pace, society is putting its stamp of approval on practices that just several decades ago were not only frowned upon but were outright illegal. Whereas once the Christian church had a significant impact on society, today almost every vestige of our Christian heritage is being eradicated. After spreading like wildfire from a tiny handful of believers to the four corners of the world Christianity today is in retreat at an even more rapid rate than that by which it spread.

There must be a root cause for this reversal that the Christian Church is overlooking — a fundamental flaw in our approach. Why did Christians once exert influence on both social customs and laws of government but today are finding that even in the United States, the so-called land of the free with a constitution that guarantees the free exercise of religion, their rights are being flagrantly violated?

Ken Ham gets to the bottom of the problem in this book. He shows how we have been simply fighting the symptoms of overlooking the root cause. Why have we not been able to convince the world of the evils of abortion, divorce, homosexuality, pornography, and drugs? Mr. Ham has identified the real crux of the matter. The cause is so subtle that even most of the large religious denominations have been deceived and have failed to recognize it.

With public education and even seminaries teaching that evolution, just like the law of gravity, is a scientific fact, students have decided that there must be a naturalistic explanation for everything, so they forget all about God. Anyway, they knew that His Ten Commandments put a crimp on their sexual lifestyles, so they were quite eager to escape from such constraints. They adopted the new morality; if it feels good, do anything you can get away with without being caught.

If there is no Creator, there is no purpose in life. There is thus no one watching over us to whom we must someday have to account for our actions. So we come to the root of society's problems. When God the Creator is removed from the picture, there are no absolutes; there is a loss of respect for law and absolute principles, and man is set adrift in a purposeless universe, guided only by his fickle passions and the situation of the moment.

Mr. Ham shows that Genesis in particular is a dependable account of actual events that are supported by solid scientific evidence. Furthermore, he shows how the questioning of this foundational book of the Bible, even by many Christians, has led to the degeneration of society so that the only moral codes it accepts are based upon "survival of the fittest," "do your own thing," and "if it feels good, do it." There are no moral absolutes.

This book is a must read for all Christians. It gives them much-needed answers to the common questions of the unbeliever and advice for parents who must prepare their children to face a rebellious secular world. Mr. Ham calls upon a wealth of experience in answering questions during years of lectures throughout both America and Australia.

Luther D. Sunderland
Author of *Darwin's Enigma:*
Ebbing the Tide of Naturalism

INTRODUCTION
(First Edition)

I WAS REARED IN A CHRISTIAN HOME where the Bible was totally accepted as the infallible, inerrant Word of God that provided the basis for the principles to be applied in every area of life. I recognized the conflict when as a high school student I was taught the idea of evolution. If Genesis was not literally true, then what part of the Bible could I trust?

My parents knew that evolution was wrong because it was obvious from Genesis that God had given us the details of the creation of the world. These details were important foundational truths for the rest of Christianity. At that time, the current wealth of materials now available on the creation/evolution issue was not even foreseen. I recall going to my local minister and asking him what to do about the problem. He told me to accept evolution but then add it to the Bible so that God used evolution and millions of years to bring all forms of life into being.

This was an unsatisfactory solution to the problem. If God did not mean what He said in Genesis, then how could one trust Him in the rest of the Scriptures? Not only this, but believing in evolution and millions of years meant allowing death, disease, fossils, thorns, animals eating each other, and suffering to be in existence millions of years before man! How could this be when the Bible teaches that God called His creation "very good" *before* sin? The Bible says that thorns came after the Curse and that animals (and man) were originally vegetarian. The Bible relates that man was made from dust and woman from his side. How could this correlate with man and woman evolving from ape-like creatures?

I went through my science degree and my teacher training year pigeonholing this problem, regurgitating to the lecturers what they told me concerning evolution. I did not know from a scientific perspective why I did not believe in evolution — but I knew from a biblical perspective it had to be wrong or my faith was in trouble.

Just before I received my first teaching appointment, the late Mr. Gordon Jones (who went to be with the Lord in 2012), then the associate director of a teachers' college in Australia, gave me a small book outlining some of the problems with evolution. He also told me about books that were becoming available on this topic — books authored by such people as Dr. Henry Morris. I searched the bookshops to try to collect as much of this material as possible. *The Genesis Flood* by Morris and Whitcomb was one of the first books I read on the subject. When I realized there were easy answers to the creation/evolution/millions of years dilemma, I felt a real burden from the Lord to go out and share this information with others. I call that burden a "fire in my bones," identifying with Jeremiah 20:9: "But His word was in my heart like a burning fire shut up in my bones; I was weary of holding it back, and I could not." I could not understand why the Church at that time, from what I had experienced, had not made people aware of this information — information that had really helped restore my faith in the Scriptures and set me on fire for the Lord.

Understanding the foundational nature of the Book of Genesis to all Christian doctrine was a real awakening. This book is the result of a series of messages developed so Christians could better understand the significance and relevance of Genesis, the real nature of the creation/evolution issue, and why we are living in times where we can observe the collapse of Christianity in our Western world. Over and over again, people have come to me and said that they had never realized the importance of Genesis — in fact, for many of them it meant a complete revival of their faith. Some say it was like a conversion experience all over again. This book deals with the relevance of a literal Genesis for the church and culture. I pray that it will challenge the minds and hearts of pastors, laypeople, scholars, and students alike.

INTRODUCTION
(2012)

IT HAS BEEN 25 YEARS since my first book, *The Lie: Evolution*, was published. It is remarkable that it has still remained a strong seller after all these years. As this year marks the 25th anniversary of the publication of *The Lie*, I thought it was about time to revise and update it.

As I read through the book, I was amazed to find that most of the arguments used in 1987 against evolution/millions of years and to defend a literal Genesis are still used today. But as I thought about it more, I remembered that God's Word does not change. Furthermore, the primary arguments used in this book are obtained from the Scriptures and point out the incompatibility of the Bible with evolutionary ideas.

With that in mind, I began to update and revise this book, but I wanted to keep the basic content intact and maintain the same chapter order, while also adding modern examples and making the book more current. As I read the real-life examples of conversations and conflicts with people from over 25 years ago, I could not help but think of the verse of Scripture that reads, "That which has been is what will be, that which is done is what will be done, and there is nothing new under the sun" (Eccles. 1:9). The same conflict over origins occurs today, even if some of the arguments against the authority of God's Word have changed in some ways.

I decided to delete the two appendixes in the original edition. These were included because in 1987 there was not the plethora of information that is available today to equip people with answers to the skeptical questions that are used to attack Genesis 1–11. Now there are numerous resources (books, DVDs, curricula, and more), including websites like www.AnswersInGenesis.org, which houses thousands of articles and resources with answers to virtually any question a person may have about origins.

However, I have added three new appendixes in this edition that help detail the reasoning behind the considerable changes made throughout this new edition:

1. Even though the main arguments have remained intact, the presentation of the message has greatly matured over the past 25 years. In the original edition, I outlined the foundational argument in terms of creation versus evolution. However, to help people more fully understand and explain the message, this new edition of *The Lie* now presents it as God's Word verses man's word. See appendix 1 for the details about this change.

2. The original title of the book was *The Lie: Evolution*. And, honestly, I think that 25 years ago when I saw so many in the Church compromising with evolution, I realized this was an attack on the authority of God's Word. However, as the biblical creation movement has grown and matured, we understand more clearly that biological evolution is really the symptom of what I call the "disease" of millions of years (geological and cosmological evolution). Thus, I have added considerable sections to help people understand that even if a Christian rejects evolution but accepts an old earth and universe (millions of years), they have unlocked a door to undermine biblical authority. Not only this, but to allow for death, disease, and suffering (as exhibited in the fossil record) millions of years before man sinned is an attack on the Cross — which is a serious problem. For this reason, I have changed the title of the book to *The Lie:*

Evolution/Millions of Years to better reflect the arguments. See appendix 2 for details.

3. Throughout *The Lie*, I reference a number of compromise positions on the creation account in Genesis, such as the gap theory, progressive creation, theistic evolution, the day-age view, and others. Some of the compromise positions have not changed since the original publication of *The Lie*, while others have been popularized within the last 25 years. In order to help readers understand the positions better, I have included a section that defines each position and points out the problems with it. See appendix 3 for details.

Even though I did not use the actual term *presuppositional apologetics* in the original book, this was certainly the apologetic approach I had — and have now strengthened in this 25th anniversary edition.

Genesis 3 and the Original Cover

When *The Lie* was first published in 1987, artist Marvin Ross produced the cover design. At that time, Marvin worked as a full-time artist for the Institute for Creation Research.

I really liked the cover, as it represented what I like to call "the Genesis 3 attack" of our day. In 2 Corinthians 11:3, Paul has a warning for us:

> But I fear, lest somehow, as the serpent deceived Eve by his craftiness, so your minds may be corrupted from the simplicity that is in Christ.

Let me paraphrase this for you. Paul is warning us that Satan is going to use the same attack against us (and on our children, grandchildren, friends, family, and others) as he did against Eve to get us to a position of not believing the things of God.

We need to then look carefully at that attack and understand it so we can be prepared. To do that, we have to go back to Genesis 3:1:

> Now the serpent was more cunning than any beast of the field which the Lord God had made. And he said to the woman, "Has God indeed said [Did God really say] . . ."

The first attack was on the Word of God. Satan's method was to cause Eve and Adam to doubt the Word of God, so that doubt would lead to unbelief. And that is exactly what happened.

This attack has continued unabated since Genesis 3. The Genesis 3 attacks have continued down through the ages. However, these attacks have manifested in different ways in different eras of history. For instance, Peter and Paul, when preaching on the Resurrection, would not have been asked questions about carbon dating!

The point is, down through the ages God's Word has come under attack in different ways in different periods of history, and God's people have had to deal with these attacks as they have contended for the faith. We need to be asking ourselves a question: What is the Genesis 3 attack in our era of history? What is the "Did God Really Say" attack of our day that will be used to cause people to doubt and ultimately disbelieve the Word of God?

I believe the teaching of evolution and millions of years is that attack. The focus of the main Genesis 3 attack in our day has been leveled at the first 11 chapters of the Bible. That is what *The Lie* is all about. And that is what this original cover illustration was meant to portray. A few years after the first printing, the publisher decided to change the cover but still have an illustration that represented this Genesis 3 attack. Even though I loved the original cover (and personally still think it is the best), I understood the change because certain people felt the cover was a bit too scary looking.

Of course, the Bible does not say the fruit Adam and Eve took from the forbidden tree was an apple, as has become a sort of tradition in our culture. We do not know what the fruit was. In the Creation Museum's diorama showing Eve with the fruit in her hand, the fruit looks like small red berries of some sort. We did this to make the point the Bible does not say it was an apple — in fact, the Bible gives us no description of the fruit.

However, the cover illustration does portray the fruit as something like an apple because we wanted to grab people's attention. Because of the cultural tradition that the fruit was an apple, the artist used this fruit as a symbolic illustration so people would immediately think of the temptation when Eve, and then Adam, took the fruit in disobedience to God's clear command not to do so.

How the Ministry Has Changed

Much has happened over the course of the last 25 years. As a ministry, we have been able to reach people through a growing number of mediums — and we find more new ways each year! We praise God for how the ministry has grown.

Early in our ministry, in 1994, Answers in Genesis began to hold major conferences. Today, we receive several hundred requests each year to conduct meetings.

Later in 1994, our radio program *Answers . . . with Ken Ham* began airing on 45 stations. The program was recently reformatted and is now heard on hundreds of stations (plus podcast via iTunes and also through our website).

Our website, www.AnswersInGenesis.org, now averages around a million visits each month. Not only that, but in 2006 and again this year, our website received the prestigious "Website of the Year" award from the National Religious Broadcasters, a group of 1,300 ministries.

In January 2007, AiG launched Answers Worldwide. This division trains Christian leaders around the world in creation apologetics and works to increase the number of translated materials and articles.

In May 2007 we opened the Creation Museum in the Greater Cincinnati area. The number of visitors has been tremendous (over 1.6 million and counting!), and we trust the Lord is using the ministry of Answers in Genesis and the Creation Museum to show people the truth of the gospel and the importance of a literal Genesis to the authority of God's Word. Indeed, the Creation Museum sees visitors from a number of atheist and agnostic groups, who are often at the forefront of Genesis 3 attacks on Scripture.

I pray this book will challenge you to seriously ponder the Genesis 3 attack of our day — an attack that I believe has greatly undermined the authority of Scripture and now permeates the world. I pray this revised and updated edition of *The Lie* will make the message even more powerful in challenging the Church and the culture to return to the authority of the Word of God from the very first verse.

— Ken Ham

CHAPTER I

CHRISTIANITY
IS UNDER
MASSIVE ATTACK

AFTER A CHURCH SERVICE where I gave a sermon, a young man stated, "Understanding what you taught about the importance of standing on God's Word beginning with Genesis was like a conversion experience all over again for me."

Another time after a lecture, a young man approached me and said, "What you said . . . it's suddenly like a light bulb lighting up in my head!" A young lady standing nearby stated, "I realized today that my understanding of Christianity was like starting in the middle of a movie. *You* took me back to the beginning, and now I understand what it is all about." A middle-aged man approached and said, "This information is like a key. It not only unlocks the reason as to why we have problems in society today; it's also the key to knowing how to be much more effective in witnessing for Jesus Christ. . . . Thank you."

We are living in challenging times. On the whole, our Western culture, which was permeated by Christian thinking in the past, is becoming more anti-Christian. We are seeing steady increases in gay marriage, support for abortion on demand, unwillingness to obey authorities, unwillingness to work, marriage being abandoned, clothing being abandoned, an increase in pornography, an increase in lawlessness, and aggressive marketing campaigns by atheists promoting their religion — to name but a few areas. Christians are fighting for their freedom and being labeled as the bad guys, even in a so-called Christian nation.

What has happened in society to bring about these changes? Why is it that many people are cynical and seem to be closed to the gospel when we talk about Christ? There must be some foundational reason for this change. In 1 Chronicles 12:32, we read of "the sons of Issachar who had understanding of the times." Do we have real understanding of the times we live in? Why are we seeing the collapse of Christianity in the Western world? What is the fundamental cause? What are the basic reasons for why modern society has turned more and more away from Christ?

Even in the great nation of America, with the greatest Christian influences in the world, with more Christian resources at this time than any other time in its history, we see this nation becoming less Christian every day. More each year are using the phrase "Happy Holidays" instead of "Merry Christmas." Nativity scenes, crosses, and the Ten Commandments are being banned from view in public

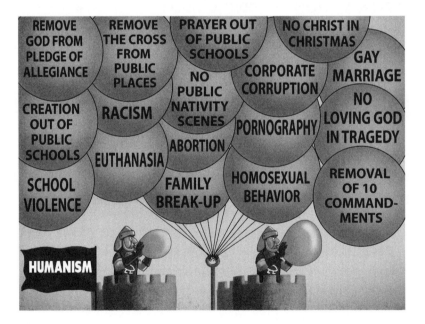

places. Creation, prayer, and the Bible have largely been eliminated from the nation's secular education system.

And for all the churches, mega-churches, and church programs, the Church is not touching the culture as it used to; I contend it is because the culture has by and large invaded the Church.

Years ago, our Western society was based largely on Christian absolutes, built on the Bible. People knew what was right and what was wrong. Behaviors such as sexual deviancy, easy divorce, public lawlessness, gay marriage, abortion on demand, pornography, and public nudity were considered to be wrong. Varying punishments for offenders were meted out by society. Moral judgments were basically built on biblical principles (for example, the Ten Commandments). Most people accepted or respected a belief in God and to a large degree, held to Christian morality.

In recent times, however, more and more people have rejected the Bible as the absolute authority on which to build one's worldview. As people have increasingly rejected belief in God's authoritative Word as the foundation for their thinking, they have also questioned the basis of the morals of the society in which they live. For instance, if there is no God, then why should they obey any of the Ten Commandments? Why should anyone say gay marriage is wrong? Why should women be barred from having abortions whenever they desire? Once people eliminate God's Word as the basis for their morality, they set about to change any laws based on Christian absolutes that held God as Creator (and thus owner) of everything.

Christian absolutes have been diluted or removed as the basis of society and replaced with a worldview that says, "We do not have to accept that the Christian way of doing things (basing our world and life views on biblical principles) is the only way; we must tolerate all religious beliefs and ways of life. We determine right and wrong." I believe we are increasingly in a situation similar to that described in the book of Judges: "In those days there was no king in Israel; everyone did what was right in his own eyes" (Judg. 21:25). When there is no absolute authority (i.e., when the Bible is not the foundation of our thinking), moral relativism permeates the culture.

We live in an era when people are demanding "tolerance" of different moral views. However, this tolerance really means an *intolerance of the absolutes of Christianity.* This false idea of tolerance has subtly undermined Christianity, and most Christians have not recognized what was really happening. Many Christians have been deceived into believing they have no right to impose their views on society. We are told, for instance, that anti-abortionists have no business impressing their particular bias on society. Have you ever heard anyone say this about the pro-abortion groups? The result is that one bias is imposed on society by the pro-abortionists — *legalized abortion* on demand! No matter what you do, you cannot avoid the fact that in these situations, one view is being imposed on someone by someone else. There is no such thing as neutrality, although many Christians become ensnared in the trap of believing there is.

In fact, in America, this false idea of neutrality, I believe, has resulted in a major problem for the Church and nation. For instance, take the issue of so-called separation of church and state. This has been used to eliminate the Bible, prayer, creation, and other Christian thinking from most of the secular education system. Most Christians have been duped into thinking that in allowing this to happen, the secular schools are now neutral places. On the contrary, the secular education system is not neutral at all.

The Bible teaches that one is either for Christ or against Him (Matt. 12:30). One walks either in light or darkness (Eph. 5:8); one either gathers or scatters (Luke 11:23). There is no neutral position. An education system is either for Christ or against Him.

When the Bible, prayer, creation, and other aspects of Christian thinking were basically eliminated from the secular education system in America, religion was not thrown out of the schools; Christianity was. And it was replaced with the religion of naturalism or atheism. One only has to open one of the main biology textbooks used in the secular education system to see how students are taught that the whole universe (including humans and all life) is explained by naturalism. The students (and 90 percent of students from church homes attend the secular schools in the United States)[1] are being indoctrinated in the religion of atheism. They are being indoctrinated against the Bible.

---

1. Ken Ham and Britt Beemer, *Already Gone: Why Your Kids Will Quit the Church and What You Can Do to Stop It,* with Todd Hillard (Green Forest, AR: Master Books, 2009), p. 170.

Secular
Presuppositions

Biblical
Presuppositions

Some have falsely believed the assertion that students can learn about God in their religion classes or at church and home — but not in science classes because this would be allowing religion in the classroom. However, if in science class students are taught that all life (including humans like themselves) is explained by natural processes — that nothing supernatural was involved — then who is the God of the religion classes or of church? It cannot be the God of the Bible, because this God is the Creator and students are told that no Creator had anything to do with anything in the universe. Thus, students are being indoctrinated against Christianity — right under the noses of their parents and pastors.

What is happening is that the world is capturing the hearts and minds of generations of kids. And whoever captures the hearts and minds of the children will rule the culture! Interestingly, after an atheist toured the Creation Museum (opened in 2007 in the Greater Cincinnati area), which walks people through the history of the world as outlined in Genesis, he said:

> For me, the most frightening part was the children's section [in the Creation Museum]. It was at this moment that I learned the deepest lesson of my visit to the Museum. . . . It is in the minds and hearts of our children that the battle will be fought.[2]

---

2. "August 10, 2009, What I learned from the Creation Museum," posted by a member of the Secular Student Alliance, http://pnrj.xanga.com/709441435/what-i-learned-from-the-creation-museum/.

God's people have to abandon this false idea of neutrality! It is causing believers to basically hand their children and the culture over to the secularists. Sadly, this idea of neutrality also invades Christian institutions.

It is like the many theological and Bible colleges that say, "We do not take a dogmatic stand on Genesis. We tolerate all views." But what happens when someone comes along and says, "Will you allow the view that says you *must* take Genesis literally?" "Oh, no!" they say. "We cannot allow that view because we tolerate all views!" In reality, they have taken a dogmatic stand to teach a dogmatic view to their students — a view that claims people do not have to take Genesis literally if they do not want to do so.

At one lecture I gave, a person said to me in an angry tone, "This is not fair. You are insisting that we take Genesis literally, that God actually took six days, that evolution is not true, and that there really was a worldwide flood. You are being intolerant of other people's views. You must show tolerance for people like me who believe God used evolution and that Genesis is only symbolic."

I then asked, "Well, what do you want me to do?"

The person replied, "You must allow other views and be tolerant of opinions different from yours."

"Well," I said, "my view is that the literal interpretation of Genesis is the right view. All other views concerning Genesis are wrong. Will you tolerate my view?"

The person looked shocked, and he hesitated. I could almost hear him thinking, *If I say yes, then I've allowed him to say you can't have another view such as mine; if I say no, then I've obviously been intolerant of his view. What do I do?* He then looked at me and said, "That's semantics!" What he really meant was that he had lost the argument and did not want to admit his intolerance of my position. The fact is, he had taken a dogmatic, closed-minded position.

Occasionally people are upset when dogmatic statements are made. They say, "You cannot be dogmatic like that." This in itself is a dogmatic statement. *Many think that some people are dogmatic and others are not. It is not a matter of whether you are dogmatic or not but of which dogma is the best dogma with which to be dogmatized!*

At one time in Australia many years ago, a group called "Toleration" began. They were insisting on a tolerance of all religious ways, beliefs, and customs. They said that we had to stop intolerance in society. In their promotional leaflet explaining their particular view, it was very interesting to note that they listed all the things they were against, and most of the things of which they were intolerant were related to Christianity. What they really meant was that they wanted a tolerance of anything in society *except Christianity. They were against the absolute authority of the Word of God.* The idea of open-mindedness comes from the notion that there is no such thing as absolute truth, or that truth cannot be absolutely known. Some say, "There are no absolutes." Ironically, this premise has become their one absolute. Such ideas are derived from an anti-biblical philosophy that holds that everything is relative.

Christian absolutes — those truths and standards of Scripture that cannot be altered — are becoming less and less tolerated in society because increasingly God's Word is no longer the foundation for building a person's worldview. Eventually this must result in the outlawing of Christianity — a possibility that seems more and more real with legislation that not only restricts Christian activities even in America but that also lays a foundation for Christians to be viewed as criminals because of the way hate crimes legislation and other laws can ultimately be used.

When Christian absolutes were the basis of society, immoral activities such as homosexual or lesbian lifestyles and abortion were outlawed. There has been a fundamental shift. Our society is now based on a relative morality: that is, a person can do what he likes and is answerable to no one but himself as long as the majority of people can be persuaded that their interests are not being threatened. This relative morality results in society being told that no one can say anything against those who choose to be sexual deviants, to be public nudists, or to do whatever they want (largely within the confines of the law, which is also changing to become more tolerant of people's actions). Yes, we even see this kind of tolerance in regard to nudity. In 2009 there was a case in Oregon in which a town was tolerating nudity within certain limits. A man decided to walk naked near three city schools, one of which was an elementary school. It was interesting to see one of the leaders for the local authority quoted in a news report:

> But Councilor Carol Voisin said she didn't think that parents' desires to protect children from seeing naked adults should trump freedom of expression. "Where does it end?"[3]

And of course, we ask the same question! Where does it end! If there are no absolutes, then all is relative; anything ultimately goes.

God's absolutes dictate that there are rules by which we must abide. Christianity cannot coexist in a world community with relative morality as its basis. One or the other will yield. There are two worldviews with two totally different belief systems clashing in our society. The real war being waged is a great spiritual war — God's Word versus autonomous human reasoning, Christian absolutes (built on the Bible) versus moral relativism (man determining his own rules). Sadly, today many Christians fail to win the war because they fail to recognize the real nature of the battle.

It is my contention that this spiritual conflict is rooted in the issue of authority — God's Word or man's word. And in this era of history, the origins issue (creation/evolution/millions of years) has had much to do with the undermining of God's Word to generations of people. Although the thought may sound strange or new to

---

3. Vickie Aldous, "Nudity Issue Sparks More City Council Debate," *Ashland Daily Tidings*, http://www.dailytidings.com/apps/pbcs.dll/ article?AID=/20091118/NEWS02/911180316.

some readers, biblically and logically the origins issue and its effect on biblical authority in the culture is central in the battle for people's souls in our culture today.

Most people have the wrong idea about what the creation/evolution/age of the earth questions involve. Instead of perceiving the real issue, they have been deceived into believing that evolution/millions of years is science and that the Bible's account of origins is religion. But this is not so (see chapter 2 for further discussion).

The word *science* basically means knowledge, and there is a big difference between knowledge gained by observation (i.e., the knowledge that helps us build our technology) and knowledge concerning the past and how the universe and life originated.[4] The origins issue concerns that second type of knowledge, belief systems about the past. We do not have access to the past. We only have the present. All the fossils, all the living animals and plants, our planet, the universe — everything exists in the present. We cannot directly test the past using the scientific method (which involves repeating things and watching them happen) since all the evidence we have is in the present.

It is important to understand that special creation, by definition, is also a belief about the past. The difference is that creationists base their understanding of creation upon a book that claims to be the *Word of the One who was there*, who knows everything there is to know about everything, and who tells us what happened. Evolution/millions of years comes from the words of men who *were not there* and who do not claim to be omniscient. This whole issue revolves around whether we believe the words of God who was there or the words of fallible humans (no matter how qualified) who were not there.

It is astonishing in this so-called scientific age that so few people know what science really is or how it works. Many, when they think of the origins issue, think of scientists as unbiased people in white laboratory coats objectively searching for the truth. However, scientists come in two basic forms, male and female, and they are just

---

4. For more information on observational science and historical science, see Roger Patterson, *Evolution Exposed* (Hebron, KY: Answers in Genesis, 2006), p. 24–26, http://www.answersingenesis.org/articles/ee/what-is-science.

like you and me. They have beliefs and biases. A bias determines what one does with the evidence, especially the way in which one decides that certain evidence is more relevant or important than other evidence. Scientists are not objective truth seekers; they are not *neutral*.

Many people misunderstand bias, thinking that some individuals are biased and some are not. Consider an atheist, for example. Such a person believes there is no God. Can atheists entertain the question, "Did God create?" The answer is no. As soon as they even allow it as a question, they are no longer atheists. So, to an atheist scientist looking at the fossils and the world around him, it would not matter what evidence he were to find. It could have nothing to do with biblical events such as Noah's Flood. Even if he found a big boat on the top of Mount Ararat, he could never allow that evidence to support the claims of the Bible regarding Noah's ark. As soon as he did, he would have abandoned his atheistic religious framework. An atheist is 100 percent biased. This should be kept in mind whenever one reads a textbook or sees a television program produced by an atheist.

Now please do not misunderstand. Evolutionists and creationists can both do great science — in regard to observational science. That is why an atheist evolutionist and a biblical creationist can both be part of a team building a space shuttle — and they will agree on how to build this technology. But they will disagree when discussing the origin of Mars or of the universe because of their biases. They both agree when it comes to observational science but disagree when it comes to origin science.

I have seen many examples of bias exhibited in various ways. I was on a talk-back radio show in Denver, Colorado, and the radio announcer said I had seven minutes to give the evidence for creation. He would just sit back and listen. So I went into detail about what the Bible says concerning Noah's Flood, the Tower of Babel, and other related topics. I explained how evidence from various cultures and from the fossil record supports what the Bible says. I explored various other aspects of creation to demonstrate the truth of the Bible. At the end of the seven minutes, the announcer made this comment on the air, "Well, I didn't hear any evidence for creation at all; so much for that!" Of course, what he meant was that he was not prepared to accept the evidence I had given him because he wanted to hold on to his own bias — agnosticism.

An agnostic is 100 percent biased. He believes one cannot know anything for sure, so no matter how much evidence he hears, he can still say, "I do not know." As soon as he knows, he has stopped being an agnostic. From a biblical perspective, Romans 1 teaches that the evidence for creation is all around us; therefore, anyone who does not believe in the Creator and Savior is condemned. It is also important to recognize that one does not have to see the Creator to recognize the fact of special creation. Just because one cannot see the architect and builder who designed and constructed a house does not mean that there was not an intelligent designer behind it.

But what about a revelationist — that is, a person who believes that the God of history has revealed the truth about Himself by means of a book? (A book that claims over 3,000 times to be the Word of God.) Can such a person consider the opposite question, that God did *not* create? No! Because he starts with the premise that God is Creator and His word is true.

Atheists, agnostics, and revelationists (and theists) hold to religious positions; and what they do with the evidence will again be determined by the assumptions (beliefs) of their religious positions. *It is not a matter of whether one is biased or not. It is really a question of which bias is the best bias with which to be biased.* That is why at the Creation Museum, one of the first exhibit rooms is called the Starting Points room. A series of signs teaches people that we all have a starting point on which to build our worldview — and ultimately there are only two starting points. We either start with the Word of One who has always been there, who knows everything, and who reveals to us the truth of the past so we can correctly understand the present or we start with ideas of fallible man, who has not always been there and who does not know everything.

Glaring examples of bias can be seen in public education in response to creation ministry. The following conversation, which is rather typical of students in the public school system, shows what bias is all about. After a presentation on creation, one student stated, "There is no way Noah's ark could be true; he couldn't have fit all the animals on board." I then asked the student, "How many animals would he have needed to put on board?" The student gave the usual reply: "I don't know, but it certainly couldn't have happened." I then asked him, "How big was the ark?" Again he answered, "I don't know, but he couldn't have fit the animals on board." In other words, here was a student who did not know how big Noah's ark was or how many animals God would have needed to put on board, but he had already decided it is a fairy tale that could not have happened.

At one town an enthusiastic supporter of our creation ministry told how he had spoken to fellow academics at a local university concerning Noah's Flood. They, of course, mocked and scoffed at the idea. He then mentioned that someday someone might find Noah's ark on Mount Ararat.[5] One fellow academic turned to him and said that even if they found a big boat that looked like Noah's ark on the top of Mount Ararat and dragged it to the main street of the city, he would still refuse to believe it. His bias was showing.

There have been many occasions where I have been able to give a convincing and logical presentation to the students. Many of them then looked to their teachers to try to make some point that could demonstrate where I was wrong. It is easy to read the expressions on the students' faces. Their expressions seem to say that this all sounds convincing, but surely there must be something wrong with it because they really do not want to believe that the Bible is true. A teacher may respond by asking a question that sounds to the students as if the teacher has proven me wrong. In the students' eyes, there is no way I would be able to answer the question. Often students spontaneously break into applause (their way of rejoicing over what they think is my demise). However, it is interesting to watch their faces and see their jaws drop when I am able to give a reasonable answer to the question; they are back where they started. It is sad that, for many of them, they have already made up their minds and decided they really do not want to believe the Bible.

I am often asked how people change their biases. This is a good question. As a Christian, the only way I can answer is to say that in this

5. For more information on Noah's ark and the Flood, see Ken Ham and Tim Lovett, "Was There Really a Noah's Ark and Flood?" in *The New Answers Book 1*, Ken Ham, editor (Green Forest, AR: Master Books, 2006).

area it has to be a work of the Holy Spirit. The Bible teaches that we walk in either the light or in darkness (Acts 26:18), gather or scatter, are *for* Christ or *against* Him (Matt. 12:30). The Bible clearly declares that no person is neutral and that each one does have a bias. We are all dead in trespasses and sin. Our very nature is that we are against God. Since it is the Holy Spirit who convicts the world of sin (John 16:8) and convinces people of the truth through the proclamation of the Word of God, then it is only through the work of the Holy Spirit and the Word of God that our biases can change. As Christians, our job is to bring the Word of God (which is sharper than any two-edged sword) to people in a clear and gracious way and pray that the Spirit might use what we say (as we honor God's Word and give reasons to defend our faith) to open hearts and minds to Christ. I believe Christians understand bias better than others. All Christians were once lost sinners biased against God. They have seen how Jesus Christ can change their bias as He transforms their lives through the power of His Spirit.

One of the reasons why creationists have such difficulty in talking to certain evolutionists is because of the way bias has affected the way they hear what we are saying. Some evolutionists already have preconceived ideas about what creationists do and do not believe. They have prejudices about what they want to understand in regard to our scientific qualifications and so on.

There are many examples of evolutionists who have totally misunderstood or misinterpreted what creationists are saying. They hear us through their evolutionary/millions of years ears, not comprehending in the slightest the perspective from which we are coming. As biblical creationists, we understand that God created a perfect world, man fell into sin, the world was cursed, God sent Noah's Flood as judgment, and Jesus Christ came to die and be raised from the dead to restore all things. In other words, our message is one of creation, Fall, and redemption. At the Creation Museum, we summarize biblical history as the Seven C's of History — Creation, Corruption, Catastrophe, Confusion, Christ, Cross, and Consummation.[6] However, because

---

6. For a more detailed description of the Seven C's of History, see Stacia McKeever, "What is a Biblical Worldview?" in *The New Answers Book 2*, Ken Ham, editor (Green Forest, AR: Master Books, 2008), http://www.answersingenesis.org/articles/nab2/what-is-a-biblical-worldview.

evolutionists are used to thinking in uniformitarian terms (i.e., basically the world we see today — the world of death and struggle — has gone on for millions of years), they do not understand this creationist perspective of history.

An interesting example came up in a debate between Dr. Gary Parker and a professor from LaTrobe University in Victoria, Australia. One of the evolutionist's refutations of creation centered on his assertion that there were too many imperfections in the world to have been made by a Creator. This particular evolutionist would not understand, even after it was clearly presented, that the world we are looking at today is not the same world God created because of the effects of the Fall and the Flood. To understand the creation/evolution/age of the earth issue correctly, one must have a complete understanding of the beliefs adhered to by both biblical creationists and secular evolutionists.

In another example, an evolutionist biologist said that if God made all the animals during the fifth and sixth days of creation, why do we not find parakeets and mice in the Cambrian strata alongside trilobites? Dr. Parker explained that parakeets and mice do not live in the same environment as the trilobites. He also explained to this scientist that the fossil record should be seen in terms of the sorting action of a worldwide flood.[7] Because animals and plants live in different areas, they would have been trapped in sediments representative of their particular environment. Again, we see bias causing one of misunderstandings that so many have of the creationist position.

The reader needs to be aware that, when discussing creation/evolution and the age of the earth, we are talking about beliefs of two different religions — religions that have two different starting points: God's Word or man's word. The controversy is not religion versus science, as the evolutionists try to make out. It is religion versus religion, the science of one religion versus the science of

---

7. For more information on fossils and the fossil record, see Andrew Snelling, "Doesn't the Order of Fossils in the Rock Record Favor Long Ages?" in *The New Answers Book 2*, Ken Ham, editor (Green Forest, AR: Master Books, 2008), http://www.answersingenesis.org/articles/nab2/do-rock-record-fossils-favor-long-ages.

the other — God's word versus man's word. Or, as we will discuss later on, God's account of historical science versus man's account of historical science.

Now it is true that creationists and evolutionists both use observational science in their efforts to defend their beliefs. For example, evolutionists use natural selection as supposed evidence for a Darwinian process. However, creationists agree that natural selection occurs, but they point out that this is not a mechanism to change one kind of animal into a totally different kind. It only operates on the genetic information already available within each kind. Thus, one can observe different species within each kind — but that only confirms that animals and plants exist in groups (or kinds). A kind is in most instances similar to the *family* level of classification.

The idea of molecules-to-man evolution is a religious position that makes human opinion supreme.[8] As we shall see, its fruits (because of the rejection of God the Creator and Lawgiver) are lawlessness, immorality, gay marriage, abortion, racism, and the mocking of God. To be clear, evolutionary ideas themselves are not the cause of such things; note the use of the word *fruits*. But the more people believe in evolution and millions of years, and the more they reject the Bible as absolute truth, the more they will do what is right in their own eyes. In other words, moral relativism permeates their thinking.

Belief in creation (the creation account as recorded in Genesis) is a religious position based on the Word of God, and its fruits (through God's Spirit) are love, joy, peace, patience, kindness, goodness, faithfulness, gentleness, and self-control (Gal. 5:22–23). In other words, when one builds one's thinking on the Bible, then there are moral absolutes because the Bible is the Word of God, who is the absolute authority and who sets the rules and determines right and wrong. The creation/evolution/age of the earth issue and its effects on people's attitude toward biblical authority (i.e., is God's Word the absolute

---

8. Molecules-to-man evolution is what I call the evolutionary idea of one kind changing into another, such as the dinosaur kind changing into the bird kind. Molecules-to-man evolution is different from variation within a kind. For example, the different species of dogs we see are still all part of the one dog kind (dog family).

authority?) is the crux of the problems in our society today. It is the fundamental issue with which Christians must come to grips. We need to understand the times we live in and that the fundamental battle is God's Word versus man's word. The origins issue of our day has been the way that this attack on the foundation of biblical authority has been manifested.

CHAPTER 2

EVOLUTION AND RELIGION

THE TERM *EVOLUTIONIST* is used extensively throughout the following chapters. In other parts of this book, we will discuss the ideas of Christians who try to marry the concepts of evolution (biological, cosmological, and geological evolution) and the Bible. However, because the majority of evolutionists are not Christians, I wish the reader to understand that the term *evolutionist* is used to mean those who believe that molecules-to-man evolution (biological evolution) — in the sense of time, chance, and struggle for survival (naturalism) — is responsible.

The term *evolution* is also used extensively throughout this book. When most people hear the word *evolution*, they typically think of biological (molecules-to-man) evolution. However, the word *evolution* can also mean cosmological evolution (i.e., the supposed big bang is the origin of the universe) or geological evolution (i.e., the supposed millions of years taken to lay down the fossil-bearing sedimentary rock layers). When the word *evolution* is used in this book, in most cases it will mean biological evolution (though even biological evolution assumes geological and cosmological evolution).

The autumn 1985 (vol. 2, no. 5) issue of *The Southern Skeptic* (the official journal of the South Australian branch of the Australian Skeptics, whose aims are similar to American humanist groups) devoted its entire 30 pages to an attack on the creation apologetics ministry in Australia and the United States. On the last page, we read the following: "Even if all the evidence ended up supporting whichever scientific theories best fitted Genesis, this would only show how clever the old Hebrews were in their use of common sense, or how lucky. It does not need to be explained by an unobservable God."

Much more recently, Richard Dawkins, during a debate with Cardinal George Pell, was asked by the moderator what kind of proof would change his mind about God's existence. Dawkins indicated in his response that even if a "great big giant 900-foot-high Jesus . . . strode in and said, 'I exist. Here I am,' " his mind likely still would not be changed.[1]

These people who vehemently attack the biblical creation ministry on the grounds that we are a religious group are themselves a religious group. They have really said that even if all the evidence supported the Book of Genesis, they still would not believe it was an authoritative document. They are working from the premise (their starting point) that the Bible is not the Word of God, nor can it ever be. They believe, no matter what the evidence, that there is no God. Thus, whatever evidence they consider, they always interpret this evidence in relation to the past (the origins issue) from the starting point of denying that the Bible's account of origins is relevant in any way. These same people are most adamant that evolution (biological, cosmological, and geological) is a fact.

I wrote in the first chapter that there is not neutral ground when it comes to our beliefs and our starting points. Consider this recent news story. In January 2012, a woman who practices witchcraft challenged the distribution of Bibles by the Gideons International at her son's public school. She stated, "Schools should not be giving out one religion's materials and not others."[2] Ultimately, she either wanted

---

1. Richard Dawkins and George Pell, interview by Tony Jones, *Q&A: Adventures in Democracy*, ABC1 (Australia), April 9, 2012, http://www.abc.net.au/tv/qa-nda/txt/s3469101.htm.

2. Jonathan Serrie, "Pagan Mom Challenges Bible Giveaway at North Carolina School," Fox News, http://www.foxnews.com/us/2012/01/18/pagan-mom-challenges-bibles-in-north-carolina-school/.

pagan spell books given away to students or the Bibles removed from the school. She did not want a religion that starts with God's Word being promoted over a religion that does not. But there is a larger problem with this story. There is already a religion being promoted and taught in our public schools: the religion of evolution.

We need to understand that there is a belief (religious) aspect to evolution. We also need to understand that there is an observable science aspect to what evolutionist scientists discuss in regard to this topic.

Let me explain. The root meaning of the word *science* is basically that of knowledge:

> The state of knowing; knowledge as distinguished from ignorance or misunderstanding.[3]

However, most people do not understand that there are two types of science (knowledge) covered when discussing the origins issue — historical science (one's account of the past) and observational science (knowledge gained by direct observation; this type of science has enabled technological progression). Christians and non-Christians, creationists, and evolutionists all have the same observational science (known as empiricism and based on repeatable tests), but they have different historical science (different beliefs about the past — about our origins).

Usually what happens in our culture is that evolutionists mix historical and observational science together and call it *science*. One has to learn to separate these out to understand which is belief (interpretation) and which is observed. For instance:

1. When a scientist classifies rocks as igneous, metamorphic, or sedimentary, that is observational science. But if the

---

3. *Merriam-Webster's Collegiate Dictionary*, 11th ed., s.v. "Science."

same scientist then claims that rocks are millions of years old, that is historical science.

2. Observing speciation as the result of what is called natural selection is an example of observational science. But scientists who insist this is evidence of evolution have now stepped into the arena of historical science — their belief that this is a mechanism for evolution.

3. Observing an element in a laboratory changing as a result of radioactive decay would come under the heading of observational science. But using a number of unverified assumptions and extrapolating backward in time to use radioactive decay to supposedly determine the age of a rock is historical science.

It is important to understand that there are highly respected scientists who believe in evolution. They could be scientists who help build the space shuttle or put the rover on Mars. Their observational science and the resulting technology is something we can all applaud — and we even honor them for their great scientific achievements. But if the same scientists then begin to make statements about millions of years in regard to the rocks on Mars, they have stepped into the area of historical science.

However, the belief aspect of atheistic evolution (the historical science) is based on a religious philosophy — a philosophy that claims this process happened naturally and that the Bible's account of origins is not valid.

Biblical creationists are up front in explaining to people that both creation and evolution have observational science aspects (in fact, the same observational science), but they have totally different historical science aspects (different beliefs — religions — concerning origins).

The differing religious views of life determine how people build their particular worldview through which they view the universe and determine their actions. The origins debate is not, therefore, one of science versus religion but one of religion (belief or starting point) versus religion (belief or starting point). Observational science can be used to confirm or refute one's starting point. Creation scientists are adamant that observational science overwhelmingly confirms the historical account of creation, the Flood, and the Tower of Babel in the Bible — and that it does *not* confirm evolution.

The famous evolutionist Theodosius Dobzhansky quotes Pierre Teilhard de Chardin: "Evolution is a light which illuminates all facts, a trajectory which all lines of thought must follow."[4] To the Christian, of course, this is a direct denial of the sayings of Jesus as quoted in John 8:12: "I am the light of the world. He who follows Me shall not walk in darkness, but have the light of life." In Isaiah 2:5 we are exhorted to "walk in the light of the LORD." In verse 22 of the same chapter we read, "Sever yourselves from such a man, whose breath is in his nostrils."

It does not take much effort to demonstrate that the belief aspect of evolution, observational science, involves, of course, observation, using one or more of our five senses (taste, sight, smell, hearing, touch) to gain knowledge about the world and to be able to repeat the observations. Naturally, one can only observe what exists in the present. It is an easy task to understand that no scientist was present over the suggested millions of years to witness the supposed evolutionary progression of life from the simple to the complex. No living scientist was there to observe the first life forming in some primeval sea. No living scientist was there to observe the big bang that is supposed to have occurred 15 billion years ago, nor the supposed formation of the earth 4.57 billion years ago — or even 10,000 years ago! No scientist was there; no human witness was there to see these events occurring. They certainly cannot be repeated today.

The same, of course, can be said of the Bible's account of origins. No human being in the present was there to observe creation, the Flood, and so on. However, the difference is that the Creator God of the Bible, who was there (and has always existed), had written down for us the events of history we need to know to understand the present world.

All the evidence a scientist has exists *only* in the present. All the fossils, the living animals and plants, the world, the universe — in fact, everything — exists *now*, in the present. The average person

---

4. Theodosius Dobzhansky, "Nothing in Biology Makes Sense Except in the Light of Evolution," *The American Biology Teacher* (March 1973): p. 129.

FOSSILS EXIST IN THE PRESENT!

(including most students) is *not* taught that scientists have only the present and cannot deal directly with the past. Evolution is a belief system about the past based on the words of men who were not there but who are trying to explain how all the evidence of the present (that is, fossils, animals, and plants, and so on) originated.

Webster's Dictionary defines *religion* as follows: "a cause, principle, or system of beliefs held to with ardor and faith."[5] Surely this is an apt description of biological, cosmological, and geological evolution. Evolution is a belief system — a religion!

It only takes common sense to understand that one does not dig up an "age of the dinosaurs" supposedly existing 65 to 200 million years ago. One digs up *dead* dinosaurs that exist *now, not* millions of years ago. Fossilized bones do not come with little labels attached telling you how old they are. Nor do fossils have photographs with them telling you what the animals looked like as they roamed the earth long ago.

When people visit a museum, they are typically confronted by bits and pieces of bones and other fossils neatly arranged in glass cases. These are often accompanied by pictures representing an *artist's impression* of what the animals and plants could have looked like in their supposed natural environment. Remember, no one dug up the picture, just the fossils. And these fossils exist in the present. For example, in Tasmania there is a sandstone bed containing millions of pieces of bones, most of which are no larger than the end of your thumb. The evolutionists have placed a picture at one particular excavation so tourists can see how the animals and plants lived in the region "millions of years ago." You can stare at those pieces of bones

---

5. *Merriam-Webster's Collegiate Dictionary*, 11th ed., s.v. "Religion."

for as long as you like, but you will never see the picture the scientists have drawn. The picture is their story of their own preconceived bias, and that, ultimately, is all it ever can be.

Remember that the next time you visit a natural history museum (like the Smithsonian in Washington, DC). The evidence is often in the glass case, but the evolutionary story about what supposedly happened in the past — devised by humans who were not there — is pasted on the glass case.

When lecturing in schools and colleges, sometimes I like to ask the students what can be learned from a fossil deposit. I ask the students whether all the animals and plants contained in the deposits lived together, died together, or were buried together. I then warn them to make sure that the answer they give me is consistent with true scientific research. As they think about it, they come to realize that they do not know if the organisms lived together because they did not see it happen. They do not know if the organisms died together because they did not see that happen either. All they really know is that they are buried together (observational science) because they were found together. Therefore, if you try to reconstruct the environment in which the organisms lived (historical science), just from what you find there, you could be making a terrible mistake. The difference between historical and observational science needs to be taught in the education system! Sadly, in most instances it is not.

The only way anyone could always be sure of arriving at the right conclusion about anything, including origins, depends upon his knowing everything there is to know. Unless he knew that every bit of evidence was available, he would never really be sure that any of his conclusions were right. He would never know what further evidence there might be to discover and therefore, whether this would change his conclusions. Neither could a person ever know if he had reached the point where he had all the evidence. This is a real problem for any human being — how can anyone ever be 100 percent sure about anything? It is something of a dilemma, is it not? It is like watching a murder mystery on television. What happens? It is obvious. Halfway through, the viewer knows who did it — the butler. Toward the end, this conclusion is still obvious. Three minutes before the end, new evidence is admitted that you did not have before, and this totally changes your conclusions. It was not the butler after all!

If you have ever watched those TV shows like *NCIS, CSI,* or any other similar program, you will notice that they often involve forensic scientists trying to reconstruct how a crime occurred from the evidence they have in the present. The same limitations they have apply to scientists looking at life and the fossil record and trying to reconstruct the past. Forensic scientists love to find a witness who can help them reconstruct the crime. Evolutionists do not have an origins witness — but Christians do!

The Bible tells us that in God the Father and His Christ "are hidden all the treasures of wisdom and knowledge" (Col. 2:3). There is no way any human mind can know all there is to know. But we have someone who does. This ends our dilemma. We are in no doubt that what God has revealed in His Word is truthful and accurate. He is not a man that He should lie (Num. 23:19) about *anything.* In time, we will know more fully. He will add to our knowledge, but He will not change what His Word has already revealed. If we want to come to the right conclusions about our origins, then the correct starting point is the Word (Scriptures) of the only reliable witness (God).

No human being, no scientist, has all the evidence. That is why fallible scientists change their ideas continuously. As scientists continue to learn new things, they change their conclusions.

Secular evolutionists claim that they are true scientists because they are willing to change their conclusions when new evidence comes along. They claim that biblical creationists cannot be real scientists because their views are set by what the Bible states, and therefore biblical creationists cannot change their conclusions. However, as pointed out before, both evolutionists and creationists have a historical science (belief about what happened in the past concerning origins). Creationists admit their historical science comes from the Bible — and that account cannot be changed. But secular evolutionists have set beliefs too! They claim life can only be explained by naturalism and that the account of origins in the Bible is not true. They are not prepared to change these beliefs!

I find over and over again that biblical creationists will admit the belief aspect of their origins account, but secular evolutionists usually refuse to do this! It is all a part of how they attempt to brainwash the public by falsely labeling creation as religion and evolution as science. As stated above, both have observational and historical science aspects.

The story has been told of a person who went back to his university professor many years after completing his degree in economics. He asked to look at the test questions they were now using. He was surprised to see that they were virtually the same questions he was asked when he was a student. The lecturer then said that although the questions were the same, the answers were entirely different!

I once debated with a geology professor from an American university on a radio program. He said that evolution was real science because evolutionists were prepared to continually change their theories as they found new data. He said that creation was not science because a creationist's views were set by the Bible and therefore, were not subject to change.

I answered, "The reason such ideas change is because we don't know everything, isn't it? We don't have all the evidence."

"Yes, that's right," he said.

I replied, "But we will never know *everything*."

"That's true," he answered.

I then stated, "We will always continue to find new evidence."

"Quite correct," he said.

I replied, "That means we can't be *sure* about *anything*."

"Right," he said.

"That means we can't be sure about evolution."

"Oh, no! Evolution is a fact," he blurted out.

He was caught by his own logic. He was demonstrating how his view was determined by his bias or starting point.

Models built upon one's starting point are subject to change for both creationists and evolutionists. The problem is that most secular scientists do not realize (or do not want to admit) that it is the belief (or religion) of evolution that is the basis for their interpretations or stories used to attempt an explanation to connect the present evidence to the past. But even if secular scientists do not realize or want to admit this, others can see that evolution is clearly a religion. A few years ago, I received an e-mail from someone who had visited the Creation Museum:

> As a businessman, I have to come to understand a little about the power of corporate branding. Evolution has done an incredible job of branding itself as science. In reality, the theory of evolution is nothing more than packaged, man-made religion, a bit like a poor product masked in savvy and interesting wrapping yet highly disappointing when opened and discovered for what it really is. In contrast, the Creation Museum and the teachers and scientists who support it are sharing timeless and unchangeable truths as revealed in God's Word. . . . Creationists, many of whom are highly educated and experienced teachers and scientists with a reverence and saving knowledge of God, are those whom we can look to for answers because, by God's grace in their lives, they know where the answers originate. Such answers have never been found in the slick wrapping of man-induced theory but always from the Creator of science and life itself.

This person understood that the evidence is interpreted differently based on one's starting point and that evolution is really just a belief system secular scientists use to interpret the evidence. Secular evolutionists are not prepared to change their actual belief that all life can be explained by natural processes and that no God is involved (or even needed). Evolution is really the religion to which they are committed. Christians need to wake up to this. *Evolution (whether geological, biological, or cosmological) is a religion — a way to supposedly explain the universe and life without God!*

CHAPTER 3

CREATION
AND RELIGION

BIBLICAL CREATION IS BASED on the Genesis account of origins from the Word (the Bible) of the One who is a witness of past events — who has always been there (and who is, in fact, outside of time). He moved men by His Spirit to write His words so we would have an adequate basis for finding out and understanding all we need to know about life and the universe.[1] We need to define in detail what we mean by the biblical creationist view.

This consists of basically a threefold view of history — a perfect creation, corrupted by sin, to be restored by Jesus Christ. This account is divided into seven periods, what we call the Seven C's: Creation, Corruption, Catastrophe, Confusion, Christ, Cross, and Consummation. A summary of the basic concepts follows:

1. Creation: In six days God created the heavens, the earth, and all that is in them from nothing. Each part is designed to work with all the others in perfect harmony.

---

1. For more information about the biblical canon, see Brian Edwards, "Why 66?" in *The New Answers Book 2*, ed. Ken Ham (Green Forest, AR: Master Books, 2008), http://www.answersingenesis.org/articles/nab2/why-sixty-six.

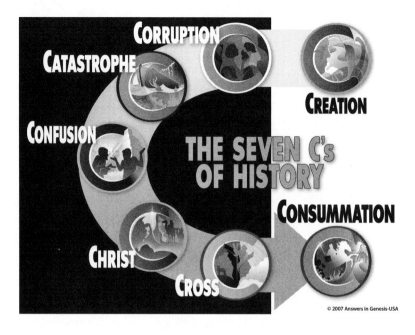

© 2007 Answers in Genesis-USA

God created the different kinds of plants and animals, and He made a special garden (the Garden of Eden) in which He created the first two human beings — Adam and Eve (Adam from dust and Eve from Adam's side — the first marriage). When God completed His work of creation, He called it all "very good." There was no death of *nephesh* creatures (*nephesh* is the Hebrew word referring to the life principle, or soul). People and animals were all vegetarian.

2. Corruption: However, we no longer live in the world God originally created. Because our first parents (Adam and Eve) placed human opinion above God's Word (as we continue to do), struggle and death entered the world, and God cursed the creation. Charles Darwin called this struggle to the death natural selection and offered his idea as a substitute for the Creator. Evolutionists later added accidental changes in heredity (mutations) to their evolutionary belief. But such processes as natural selection and mutations do not create; instead, they bring disease, defects, and decay into the world God created. Paul describes this now fallen world in

Romans 8:22: "For we know that the whole creation groans and labors with birth pangs together until now."

Because we sinned in Adam (he was the head of the human race, and we inherit his sin nature), we were cut off from God — and would be for eternity. But God had a plan to rescue us from what our sin did. In the Garden of Eden, God killed an animal and clothed Adam and Eve (Gen. 3:21). This was the first blood sacrifice and a picture of what was to come in Jesus Christ, the Lamb of God who came to take away the sins of the world. God promised this Savior in Genesis 3:15: "And I will put enmity between you and the woman, And between your seed and her Seed; He shall bruise your head, and you shall bruise His heel."

3. Catastrophe: After mankind's sin and rebellion (the Fall), the earth became so filled with violence and corruption that God destroyed that world with a global Flood and gave it a fresh start with Noah, his family, and the animals in the ark. Fossils — billions of dead things buried in rock layers laid down by water all over the earth — remind us of God's judgment on sin. Most of the fossil record is actually the graveyard of the Flood that occurred about 4,300 years ago.[2] However, this same fossil record is used by secularists as supposed evidence for millions of years.

4. Confusion: In Genesis 11, we see that after the Flood, man disobeyed God's command to spread out over the earth. Instead, they congregated together to build a tower to the heavens, likely to worship the heavens instead of worshiping and obeying the God who made the heavens.[3] As a result, God confused their language so that groups began speaking in different languages. Family groups then began separating

---

2. For more information on how the fossil record confirms the biblical account of the Flood, see Andrew Snelling, "The World's a Graveyard: Flood Evidence Number Two," *Answers*, April–June 2008, p. 76–79, http://www.answersin-genesis.org/articles/am/v3/n2/world-graveyard.

3. For more on the rebellion at Babel, see Mike Matthews, "The World in Revolt: Understanding the Rebellion at Babel," Answers, April–June 2008, p. 25–28, http://www.answersingenesis.org/articles/am/v3/n2/world-in-revolt.

from each other and moving out over the earth to develop various people groups, which resulted in the diverse cultures and nations we have today.

5. Christ and Cross: We find that the earth again became filled with violence, corruption, and death because of human sin putting man's opinion above God's Word. God had a plan from eternity promised back at the beginning (Gen. 3:15) to save man from sin and its consequence of eternal separation from God. God's Son stepped into human history to become Jesus Christ, the God-man. Fully God and fully human, Christ came to heal and restore, and by His death and Resurrection, He conquered death. We may be born again into eternal life as new creations in Christ. As Romans 10:9 tells us, "If you confess with your mouth the Lord Jesus and believe in your heart that God has raised Him from the dead, you will be saved."

6. Consummation: As surely as God created the world and judged the world with the Flood, our ungodly world will be destroyed by fire (2 Peter 3:10). For those who trust in Jesus, however, there awaits eternal life in the new heavens and the new earth. There will be no more corruption because God's Curse will have been removed. But for those who reject God's free gift of salvation, the Bible tells us they will suffer a second death — eternal separation from God (Rev. 20:14).

The Bible tells us that God knows everything. He has all knowledge. This means the Bible is the Word of someone who knows everything there is to know about the past, the present, and the future. If we want to come to right conclusions about anything, the only sure way is to start with the Word of the One who has absolute knowledge. *We Christians must build all of our thinking in every area on the Bible. We must start with God's Word, not the word of finite, fallible man. We must judge what people say on the basis of what God's Word says — not the other way around.*

At one seminar, I stated that we must build all of our thinking upon God's Word. That must be our starting point. One minister, in a rather irate manner, made the comment that this would mean he should be able to go to the Bible to find out how to fix his car. But the minister's comment was erroneous because the Bible is primarily a book of history! It is not a book that is meant to deal with observational science. It mainly deals with historical science.

Obviously, he did not understand that the principles that govern our thinking in every area must come from the Scriptures. These principles are immutable. The Bible certainly does not con-

tain the details on how to fix a car. On the other hand, modern science, which enabled the development of the car, arose when people began to base their observational science upon biblical principles (e.g., the laws of logic, the laws of nature, the uniformity of nature). Therefore, a machine (like a car) runs according to the laws that God made.

We should be able to investigate these laws God made and apply them in different areas. No informed evolutionist would question the fact that modern science arose from a biblical foundation. In other words, what we believe and how we think depends upon the basis with which we start. The Bible gives us the very foundational principles and details necessary to develop correct thinking in every area.

Unfortunately, too many people have started with the words of fallible humans and then judged what the Bible states. For example, some have taken man's belief in millions of years as truth and then reinterpreted God's clear Word in Genesis concerning creation in six literal days!

What an arrogant position this actually is! We cannot tell God what He should say. We must be prepared to come totally under His authority and listen to what He says to us.

If the Bible is not the infallible Word of the One who knows everything, then we can never know for sure that we can come to right conclusions concerning the origins issue. Ultimately, we could never be sure about what this universe and life is all about. What then is truth: my word, your word, or someone else's word? In fact, how do we determine what truth is or how to search for it? In John 18:38, a man called Pilate asked, "What is truth?" Yet he was speaking in this passage to the One who said, "I am the way, the truth, and the life. No one comes to the Father except through Me" (John 14:6).

I recall a seminar where a young man stated, "I can't believe in creation. I believe in the big bang. We are just products of chance and random processes. There is no God. What do you say to that?"

I replied, "Well, if you are a product of chance, your brain is also a product of chance. Therefore, the thought patterns that determine your logic are also products of chance. If your logic is the result of chance processes, you can't be sure it evolved properly. You can't be sure you're even asking the right question because you can't trust your own logic."

He was dumbfounded. Afterward he came up and asked for the best books on the subject and said he would have to seriously think this through. He had begun to realize that, without an absolute (God), he really had nothing; life did not make sense.

As stated, the Bible is primarily a book about historical science (history — the past, including our origins). However, just as we discussed in regard to those who believe in evolution, when dealing with the topic of origins, creationists also use both historical and observational science.

We can take what the Bible says about history and see if the evidence of the present does fit. If we take the book of Genesis, which is a detailed account of our origins, we can see what it says concerning how the world was created and what subsequently happened. We can decide what we would expect to find if the Bible is true (this is our worldview, or model, built on the creation account). Then we can look at the world to see if what we observe confirms the account in God's Word (and it does, over and over again).

For example, we are told that God created living things "after their kind" (Gen. 6:20, 7:14). We can postulate, therefore, that animals and plants should be found in groups or kinds, and that one kind cannot change into a totally different kind (as proposed by evolutionists, i.e., molecules-to-man evolution).[4] In fact, this is exactly what we

---

4. For more information on the biblical kinds, see Georgia Purdom and Bodie Hodge, "Zonkeys, Ligers, and Wolphins, Oh My!" Answers in Genesis, http://www.answersingenesis.org/articles/aid/v3/n1/zonkeys-ligers-wholphins.

do find (in living as well as fossil organisms) — animals and plants exist in groups or kinds. Creationist researchers believe that in most instances, the biblical kind would be equivalent to the family level in the classification system biologists use. There can be different genera and species within a family, but such changes only occur within a kind. There are distinct boundaries that cannot be crossed. Creation scientists have written many articles about the fact that speciation and what is called "natural selection" (or adaptation) is observed, but it has nothing to do with molecules-to-man evolution. In fact, properly understood, such changes are the opposite of those needed for molecules-to-man evolution. This example of observational science confirms the Bible's account of created kinds, but it is evidence against Darwinian evolution.[5]

Genesis tells us that because of man's wickedness, God judged the world with a worldwide Flood. If this is true, what sort of evidence would we find? We could expect that we would find billions of dead things (fossils) buried in rock layers, laid down by water and catastrophic processes over most of the earth. This is exactly what we observe. Observational science confirms the Bible's historical science.

In Genesis 11, we read of the events that occurred at the Tower of Babel. Again, we can ask the question: If this event really happened, what evidence would we expect to find? Does the evidence from the cultures throughout the world fit with this? Again, the answer is overwhelmingly yes. All humans can interbreed and produce fertile offspring; we are all the same kind. The Human Genome Project in 2000 established that all humans belong to one race:

> Dr. Venter and scientists at the National Institutes of Health recently announced that they had put together a draft of the entire sequence of the human genome, and the researchers had unanimously declared, there is only one race — the human race.[6]

---

5. For more on natural selection versus evolution, see Roger Patterson, *Evolution Exposed* (Petersburg, KY: Answers in Genesis, 2006), p. 57–62, http://www. answersingenesis.org/articles/ee/natural-selection-vs-evolution.

6. Natalie Angier, "Do Races Differ? Not Really, Genes Show," *New York Times*, http://www.nytimes.com/2000/08/22/science/do-races-differ-not-really-genes-show.html?pagewanted=all&src=pm.

The results of the Human Genome Project are an example of observational science confirming the Bible's history. After all, if we really are all descendants of one man and one woman, as the Bible clearly states, then there would be only one biological race!

Sadly, Darwin proposed the idea of different races that had evolved to different levels, with what he called "Caucasians" being the supposed highest race.

One of the main biology textbooks used in American public schools in the early 1900s was based on Darwin's ideas. The 1914 edition, which was in use in 1925 during the Scopes trial, defined the races under the heading "The Races of Man":

> At the present time there exist upon the earth five races
> . . . the highest type of all, the Caucasians, represented by the
> civilized white inhabitants of Europe and America.[7]

The term *races* can be used in various ways depending upon the way it is defined. At the time of Thomas Jefferson (a founding father and the third president of the United States), the term *races* was used in reference to the Irish race, the English race, and so on. In other words, it meant a particular ethnic group. Sadly, because of the influence of Darwin's false ideas about primitive and advanced races (or lower and higher races), when people use the word *race* today, it is often interpreted in an evolutionary sense (i.e., lower and higher races).

I believe the intense evolutionary indoctrination through the educational system has fueled racism and prejudice against certain groups. In America, there is no doubt such racism exists in regard to skin "color." Consider the issue of so-called interracial marriage. A few years ago, a major news network reported on a couple that allegedly was refused their marriage license by a justice of the peace — because they had two different shades of skin color![8] Answers in Genesis has always taught that biologically there is only one race (Adam's race). Biologically, there is no such thing as interracial marriage since there is only one race.

---

7. George William Hunter, *A Civic Biology Presented in Problems* (New York: American Book Company, 1914), p. 196.

8. Samira Simone, "Governor Calls for Firing of Justice in Interracial Marriage Case," CNN, http://www.cnn.com/2009/US/10/16/louisiana.interracial.marriage/index.html.

And scientific research has established that all humans have the same basic skin color. (Genetics reveals that all skin colors are differing shades of the one main color — a pigment called melanin.) Again, observational science confirms the Bible's history that all humans are related and are descended from one man; we are all one race.

Because of the influence of evolution, Christians should use a term like *people groups* in regard to humans, not the evolutionized term *races*. As God's Word states, "And He has made from one blood every nation of men to dwell on all the face of the earth, and has determined their preappointed times and the boundaries of their dwellings" (Acts 17:26).[9]

If all humans had the same ancestor, Noah (and ultimately Adam), then all cultures have developed since Noah's Flood and the division at the Tower of Babel.

It is known that nearly every culture in the world has stories or legends from which, in a sense, one could almost write the book of Genesis. Most cultures have a story about a worldwide flood similar to Noah's Flood. Many cultures have creation legends also, which are not dissimilar to the account in Genesis regarding the creation of woman, the entrance of death, and the original man and animals being vegetarian (Gen. 1:29–30). Such accounts abound in cultures around the world. This is powerful evidence that these stories have been handed down generation after generation. The true accounts are in the Bible, but the similarities in cultures around the world are not what we would expect from the viewpoint of an evolutionary belief system. They are consistent with and confirm the biblical account of creation, the Fall, and the Flood. As people dispersed from the Tower of Babel, they took the accounts of creation and the Flood with them — but over time, they changed the accounts, resulting in elements similar to the biblical account but with all sorts of embellishments and fictions that were not part of the original accounts. The original record, which has not changed, is in the Bible.

---

9. For more on the biblical view of race, see Ken Ham and Charles Ware, *One Race One Blood: A Biblical Answer to Racism* (Green Forest, AR: Master Books, 2010).

I recall being taught at the university I attended that the reason the Babylonians (and others) had stories similar to Genesis was because the Jews had borrowed myths of Babylonian origin to include with their writings. However, when this idea is closely investigated, we find that the Babylonian stories are rather grotesque and quite unbelievable in almost every aspect. For instance, Babylonian stories concerning the Flood, like the *Atrahasis* epic or the *Epic of Gilgamesh*, portray the gods fighting over means to control the overpopulation of humanity, resulting in a worldwide flood — and a multi-story, cube-shaped ark, which would not have floated or survived a worldwide flood.[10]

When we read the biblical account of the Flood, it is certainly the believable account because it is the original one. When one thinks about it, stories handed down generation after generation that are not carefully preserved — particularly if they are handed down by word of mouth — do not improve with age. The truth is lost, and the stories degenerate markedly. The biblical records have been handed down in written form, carefully preserved by the superintendency of God, and have not been corrupted. The Babylonian stories, which only reflect the true record of the Bible, are the ones that have become corrupted, due to the limitations of human fallibility. The truth of the matter is that what happened is the opposite of what the secular world (and liberal Christians) teaches concerning this subject.

Thus, starting with the Bible and working from this foundation, the observational evidence of the present should confirm the Bible's account. And it does, confirming our faith that the Bible really is the Word of God. (A number of books that detail the scientific evidence consistent with the Bible are listed at the end of this book.)

However, all of this *proves* nothing scientifically, because, in relation to the past, nothing can be proven. Neither creation *nor* evolution can be proven scientifically. Both involve historical science (belief/religion) and observational science.

Both creation and evolution in regard to origins are belief systems that result in different worldviews and thus totally different interpretations of the evidence. This is not to say that the creationist will

---

10. Nozomi Osanai, "A Comparative Study of the Flood Accounts in the Gilgamesh Epic and Genesis," Answers in Genesis, http://www.answersingenesis.org/articles/csgeg.

always have exactly the right explanation about every fact. Because the creationist does not have all available data, there will be many things that may not be able to be explained in specific terms, but nonetheless, all facts should ultimately fit into the framework as set by the biblical record.

At one church where I spoke, a scientist (in a very vocal manner) stood and told the congregation not to believe what I had said. He informed them that, as a scientist, he could show them that what had been said concerning Noah's Flood and creation was wrong. Science, in his words, had proven the Bible to be wrong.

Since he had stated publicly that he was a Christian, I asked him if he believed there was a person in history called Noah. He said that he did believe this. I asked him why. He told me that it was because he had read it in the Bible. I asked him if he believed that there had been a worldwide Flood. His answer was no. I asked him why he did not believe there was a worldwide Flood. He then went on to say it was obvious from what he called science that there could not have been a worldwide Flood — that science had proven the Bible wrong. I asked him how he could trust the Bible when it talked about Noah if he could not trust the Bible when it actually talked about Noah's Flood. I also suggested that the particular evidence he was using to say there could not have been a worldwide Flood might be interpreted in other ways. He was actually using man's historical science to claim that Bible's historical science was incorrect!

I went on to say that we do not have all the evidence and we do not know we can trust all the fallible assumptions involved in many of the techniques used for dating the earth and so on; therefore, was it not possible that his interpretations could be wrong and the Bible could be right after all? In other words, I was saying that the worldview built on the Bible's historical science enabled one to interpret the evidence correctly. He was using man's fallible historical science of millions of years to claim the Bible's account of history was wrong!

He admitted that he did not know everything and that it was possible there were assumptions behind some of the scientific methods to which he was referring. This additional information could totally change his conclusions. He admitted this was a possibility, but then he went on to say that he could not believe the Bible in all areas (e.g., Noah's Flood) until science had proven it. He obviously did not understand the difference between observational and historical science.

I accepted the Bible as the Word of God and therefore interpreted the evidence on that basis. He was accepting the Bible as containing the Word of God but subject to proof by what he called science. However, his science was not observational science. In fact, observational science in regard to geology confirms the Bible's account of the Flood because it is obvious that massive fossil-bearing sedimentary layers (found in different continents) had to be laid down catastrophically, not slowly over millions of years.

In the public school system, I tried to ensure that my students were taught a correct understanding of science and how to think logically. I taught them how take statements made by scientists and separate out what was observational science and what was historical science. That greatly helped them to think more critically and to better understand the origins issue.

However, when I first taught creation in the public schools, my approach was different. I would show the students the problems with evolution and how evidence supported the creationist view. However, when the students went to another class where the teacher was an evolutionist, the teacher would just reinterpret the evidence for them. I had been using what can be called an *evidentialist* approach — trying to use the evidence to convince students that it proved evolution false and creation true. I was mixing historical and observational science together without explaining that to the students.

I then changed methods and taught students the true nature of science — what science can and cannot do. We looked in detail at the limitations scientists have in relation to the past. I taught them that all scientists have presuppositions (beliefs, particularly in regard to historical science) that they use in interpreting the evidence. I shared with them my beliefs from the Bible concerning creation, the Fall, Noah's Flood, and other topics, and how one builds a worldview upon this framework.

I then demonstrated how, from observational science, the evidence consistently confirmed the biblical account of origins, not evolutionary beliefs about the past.

I had begun teaching from what could be called a *presuppositional* approach.[11] The difference was astounding. When students went to their other classes and their teachers tried to reinterpret the evidence, the students were able to identify for their teachers the assumptions behind what their teachers were saying. They were able to separate out the historical from the observational science. The students recognized that it was a teacher's belief system that determined the way in which he or she interpreted the evidence. They also understood that the

---

11. A *presuppositional apologetic* is an apologetic method that presupposes the truth of the entire Bible. From that basis, it seeks to show the irrationality of any competing worldview or system.

question of origins was outside of direct scientific proof.

This so perplexed some teachers that, on one occasion, a young teacher came to me and abrasively stated that I had destroyed her credibility with the students. She had taught her students that coal formed in swamps over millions of years. I had taught the students that there were different beliefs as to how coal could be formed, and that none of us had observed it forming. However, from observational science, I showed evidence (such as pine trees that do not grow in swamps in coal) that contradicted the swamp formation idea. Since this teacher had not taught the limitations of science in regard to origins and had taught her swamp idea for the formation of coal as fact, her credibility was undermined in the eyes of the students. The reason she was so angry was that she had absolutely no comeback and knew it. So did the students.

I would appeal to any who have the opportunity to teach in the area of creation/ evolution to research carefully their method of teaching. Ensure that the students

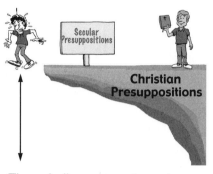

The unbeliever cannot consistently stand on his own worldview because it is irrational.

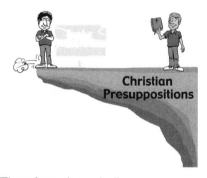

Therefore, the unbeliever must stand on the Christian worldview in order to be rational.

The unbeliever stands on Christian principles: logic, uniformity, and morality. But he denies that these are Christian principles.

understand the whole philosophical area — that is, the
presuppositions and assumptions involved. Teach them
to recognize the difference
between observational and
historical science. Not only
will students understand the
issues better, but they will
also become better scientists
and thinkers as a result.

Another existing result
of this presuppositional approach emphasizing the limi-

The unbeliever must use Christian
principles to argue against the
Bible. The fact that he is able to argue at all proves that he is wrong.

tations of science in regard to origins is the questions students ask at
the end of such a program. When using an evidential approach, the
questions and comments from students would be something like,
"What about carbon 14 dating?" "Haven't scientists proven fossils are
millions of years old?" "Surely given enough time anything can happen." However, using the presuppositional approach (which brings the
issues to the fundamental belief level), it was exciting to see a dramatic
change in the nature of the questions asked: "Where did God come
from?" "How do you know the Bible can be trusted and is true?" "Who
wrote the Bible?" "Why is Christianity better than Buddhism?" The
students started to see the real issue. It was really a conflict of two different beliefs. The results of this approach have been astounding. Many,
many students have listened to the claims of Christ and have shown
real interest in Christianity, with a number of conversions as a result.

This method works not only for public school students but for
Christian school students as well. It is also an important method for
the general public. One of the things they recognize is that creationists and evolutionists all have the same facts. Therefore, what we are
really talking about are different interpretations of these same facts.
They begin to see the real argument — two religions (two different
accounts of historical science) in conflict. Evidence is important
(which is why creationists do intensive research), but the method
used to present the evidence is vital to the success of the presentation.

After I gave a lecture to a class at a Christian college in Kansas many years ago, using material similar to that discussed already (plus additional scientific evidences), a student stated in front of the rest of the class, "What you have said sounds logical and very convincing in regard to accepting Genesis as truth. But you must be wrong because my geology professor here at the college believes in evolution and would totally disagree with you. If he were here now, I'm sure he could tell me where you are wrong, even if I can't see it at the moment." He needed to start separating out the historical science (beliefs about the past) of his professor from what is actually observed!

I replied, "Even if your geology professor were here and said things I don't understand because I'm not a geologist, if what he says about the past disagrees with the Bible, then he is wrong." In other words, his historical science (the beliefs about the past) is fallible; it is God's Word that is infallible.

I went on, "If I can't explain why he is wrong, it only means I don't have all the evidence to know the errors in his arguments." In other words, he could be making claims about how certain sediments may have formed in the past — and I might not be familiar with things he might say. A creation geologist, however, might have information from research conducted to show his claims are not verified by observational science.

I continued, "The Bible is the Word of God and is infallible. I'm sure I could get a creationist geologist to find out why your professor is wrong because the Bible will always be right!" After all, the Bible is the only infallible account of history. And there is nothing from observational science that will ever contradict God's Word.

Surely, as Christians blessed with the conviction that arises from the work of the Holy Spirit, we must accept the Bible as the infallible, authoritative Word of God. Otherwise we have nothing. If the Bible is to be questioned and cannot be trusted, and if it is continually subject to reinterpretation based on what fallible humans believe, then we do not have an absolute authority. We do not have the Word of the One who knows everything, which means we have no basis for anything. Truth is spiritually discerned. Without the indwelling of the Holy Spirit, there can be no real understanding.

CHAPTER 4

THE ROOT OF
THE PROBLEM

WHY DO EVOLUTIONISTS not want to admit that the mole-cules-to-man evolution belief is really a religion? It is related to the fact that whatever you believe about your origins affects your whole worldview, the meaning of life, and so on. If there is no God and we are the result of chance, random processes, it means there is no absolute authority. And if there is no one who sets the rules, then everyone can do whatever he likes or hopes he can get away with. As we read in Judges 21:25, "In those days there was no king in Israel; everyone did what was right in his own eyes."

Evolution is a religion that enables people to justify writing their own rules. The sin of Adam was that he did not want to obey the rules God set but instead to do his own will. He rebelled against God, and we all suffer from this same sin: rebellion against the absolute authority. The evolutionary/millions of years belief has become the so-called scientific justification in today's world for people to continue in this rebellion against God.

The Bible gives us in the Book of Genesis the true and reliable account of the origin and early history of life on earth. Increasing numbers of scientists are realizing that when you take the Bible as your basis and build your worldview upon it, then the evidence from the living animals and plants, the fossils, and the cultures fits with what this account details to us. This confirms that the Bible really is the Word of God and can be trusted completely.

The secular humanists, of course, oppose this because they cannot allow the possibility of God being Creator. They have fought successfully (sadly) to have prayer, Bible readings, and the teaching of creation forced out of the public school curriculum. They have deceived the public into thinking this is eliminating religion from schools and leaving a neutral situation. *This is simply not true!* As God's Word states, "He who is not with Me is against Me, and he who does not gather with Me scatters abroad" (Matt. 12:30).

The secularists have not eliminated religion from the public school. *They have eliminated Christianity and have replaced it with an anti-God religion — naturalism or atheism.* Consider this quote from one of the biology textbooks used in American public schools:

> Science requires repeatable observations and testable hypotheses. These standards restrict science to a search for natural causes for natural phenomena. For example, science can neither prove nor disprove that unobservable or supernatural forces cause storms, rainbows, illnesses, or cures of disease. Supernatural explanations of natural events are simply outside the bounds of science.[1]

Who decided that science could be defined this way? Those who do not believe in God and who arbitrarily defined science to eliminate the supernatural. Thus when discussing origins one can only discuss how natural processes could have brought the universe and life into existence. This is pure atheism. Even though there is a minority of Christian teachers in the public school system (and they need our prayers, as they are missionaries in a pagan system just as I once was), these schools have become, by and large, temples of atheism.

---

1. Neil A. Campbell, Brad Williamson, and Robin J. Heyden, *Biology: Exploring Life*, Florida Teacher's Edition (Upper Saddle River, NJ: Pearson Prentice Hall, 2006), p. 38.

And sadly, in America, around 90 percent of students from church homes go to this atheistic system.[2] Students do not learn apologetics in most churches and Christian homes, so they do not know how to defend the Christian faith against secular attacks. This is one of the reasons two-thirds of young people will leave the Church by college age.[3] Also, most Christian leaders sadly tell young people they can believe in evolution and/or millions of years. Young people recognize that if this is so, then they really cannot trust God's Word in Genesis — so why trust it anywhere else? This has resulted in a generational loss of the acceptance of God's Word as the absolute authority.

Most public schools have become institutions that train generations of school children in the religion of secular humanism. A minority of Christian teachers in the public school system tries to be the "salt of the earth" in such institutions. However, there are quite a number of Christian teachers who hide their light under a bushel — frightened of being consistent Christians in such a pagan environment. Some teachers have been threatened with termination of their employment if they are seen to be giving a Christian philosophy in the educational system. Others compromise evolution with God's Word — thus undermining the very authority they purport to believe in.

We see extreme emotionalism in reaction to biblical creation organizations like Answers in Genesis around the world because the evolutionists' religion is being attacked by a totally different belief system. This emotionalism can be seen in the way in which the anti-creationists talk about the issue. For instance, consider the quote from Michael Ruse (Professor of Philosophy at the Florida State University): "Scientific creationism is not just wrong; it is ludicrously implausible. It is a grotesque parody of human thought and a downright misuse of human intelligence. In short, to the Believer, it is an insult to God."[4]

2. Ken Ham and Britt Beemer, *Already Gone: Why Your Kids Will Quit the Church and What You Can Do to Stop It*, with Todd Hillard (Green Forest, AR: Master Books, 2009), p. 170.
3. Ibid., p. 21.
4. Michael Ruse, *Darwinism Defended: A Guide to the Evolution Controversies* (Menlo Park, CA: The Benjamin/Cummings Publishing Company, 1982), p. 303.

More recently, Stephen Law, senior lecturer in philosophy at the University of London, shared his emotionally charged view of creationism:

> Would I include young-earth creationism in the school curriculum anywhere at all? I might put it next to, say, some conspiracy theories as examples, as illustrations of how people can be sucked into belief systems which are utterly absurd. And yet they themselves are convinced that everyone else is wrong and they are right. Once the person becomes sucked into that kind of belief system, they're never coming out. It makes them intellectual prisoners, and they become intellectually unreachable. It also encourages them to think in ways which are, which would normally be considered symptomatic of mental illness.[5]

In a 2008 article in *The Guardian* (UK), Richard Dawkins wrote in regard to teachers who believe creation is an alternative to evolution, "We are failing in our duty to children, if we staff our schools with teachers who are this ignorant — or this stupid."[6]

The real battle is aligned with the fact that these people do not want to accept Christianity because they will not accept that there is a God to whom they are answerable. Perhaps this is why one evolutionist lecturer once said to me: "You will never convince me that evolution is religion." In other words, no matter what we were able to show him concerning the nature of evolution, he refused to accept that it was a religion. He did not want to accept that he had a faith because then he would have to admit it was a blind faith that observational science does not confirm. And he would not be able to say that it was the right faith.

The public has genuinely been misled into thinking that evolution is *only* scientific and belief in God is *only* religious. However, as I have pointed out, both have their belief aspects. Evolution is causing many people to stumble and not listen when Christians share with them the truth of the God of creation and the gospel. You will notice in

---

5. Stephen Law, "Should Creationism Be Taught in Schools?" 4thought.tv, http://www.4thought.tv/themes/should-creationism-be-taught-in-schools/stephen-law.

6. Richard Dawkins and Steve Jones, "Richard Dawkins and Steve Jones give their views on creationism teaching poll," *The Guardian*, December 22, 2008.

humanist opposition (through debates, the media, books, and so on) to biblical creation ministry that they often use *ad hominem* attacks (e.g., creationists are "anti-science," "pseudoscientific," or "anti-reality") and make emotional accusations. This is because they just cannot point to the evidence and clearly show that evolution is true! A proper understanding of the evidence contradicts the molecules-to-man evolutionary belief.

Walk into a museum and have a look at all of the supposed evidence for evolution on display. Different kinds of animals and plants are represented by carefully preserved specimens or by large numbers of fossils. You will see the story of evolution in words, or even in models constructed by artists *based on* the evolutionary belief — but not in the evidence. The evidence is *in the glass case. The hypothetical story of evolution can only be seen pasted on the glass case.*

All the evolutionists have to do is to come up with one piece of evidence that conclusively proves evolution. If evolution is right and creation is nonsense, evolutionists have the media at their disposal to prove to everyone that evolution is true. However, they cannot do this. Many documentaries are shown on TV supposedly giving evidence for evolution, but if one turns the sound off, the same evidence can be explained in terms of the biblical account of creation — and then observational science used to confirm this. The evidence overwhelmingly supports exactly what the Bible says. It is a shame that creationists do not have the same media coverage to explain to the world the overwhelming evidence for the truth of creation.

Let's face it: secular evolutionists must oppose biblical creationists because, if what we are saying is right (and it is) — that God is Creator and man is a sinner in need of salvation — then their whole philosophy is destroyed. The basis for their philosophy decrees there is no God and ultimately man is not accountable to anyone but himself. If evolution is not true, the only alternative is creation. That is why evolutionists will cling to the evolutionary philosophy of millions of years, even if the evidence is totally contradictory. It is really a spiritual question.

Some may say that if the evidence is so overwhelming that God created, surely people would believe this. In Romans 1:20 we read, "For since the creation of the world His invisible attributes are clearly seen, being understood by the things that are made, even His eternal power and Godhead, so that they are without excuse."

The Bible tells us that there is enough evidence in the world to convince people that God is Creator and to condemn those who do not believe. If that is so and the evidence is all there, why do people not believe it? Is it because they do not want to believe it? The Apostle Peter stated that in the last days men will deliberately forget that God created the world (2 Pet. 3:5). This means there is a willfulness on their part not to believe.

P.Z. Myers, associate professor of science and math at University of Minnesota–Morris, explained in a recent interview that his disbelief in God is due to a lack of evidence:

> Why don't I believe in God? Because nobody has ever shown me the evidence for it. It's a ludicrous proposition. If it were true, it would be amazing, right? It would be the most incredible thing we would ever discover in the universe — that there was some being greater than the whole of what we've been living in and studying, and he's got these vast powers — that would be earth shaking to know about. You would think if people actually had evidence for this, they would trot it out.[7]

---

7. P.Z. Myers, "God's Theme Park," *Dateline* (Australia), March 6, 2012, http://www.sbs.com.au/dateline/story/watch/id/601409/n/God-s-Theme-Park.

But we know that because Romans 1:20 says that God is clearly seen so that man is without excuse, Myers's disbelief is really a willful ignorance. We also need to make sure we never divorce Romans 10:17 from Romans 1:20. Romans 10:17 states, "So then faith comes by hearing, and hearing by the word of God."

Yes, evidence is important (1 Peter 3:15 says to "always be ready to give a defense"), but it is God's Word that convicts; it is God's Word that is sharper than a two-edged sword (Heb. 4:12). It is from God's Word that we understand we are sinners and in need of salvation. It is from God's Word that we learn about the saving gospel. Whenever we are using evidence, we should always do it in such a way as to point people to the Word of God. It is only through the Word of God that a sinner is saved.

The Bible tells us, "There is none who understands; There is none who seeks after God" (Rom. 3:11) and, "For it is the God who commanded light to shine out of darkness, who has shone in our hearts to give the light of the knowledge of the glory of God in the face of Jesus Christ" (2 Cor. 4:6). In other words, it is God who opens our hearts to the truth. When we think of the story of the pharaoh who would not let God's people leave Egypt, the Bible says, "But the LORD hardened Pharaoh's heart, and he would not let them go" (Ex. 10:27). This idea is also recorded in Exodus 7:14: "So the LORD said to Moses: 'Pharaoh's heart is hard; he refuses to let the people go.' "

In the New Testament we read that Jesus taught the Pharisees and scribes in parables: "And in them the prophecy of Isaiah is fulfilled, which says: 'Hearing you will hear and shall not understand, and seeing you will see and not perceive; for the hearts of this people have grown dull. Their ears are hard of hearing, And their eyes they have closed, lest they should see with their eyes and hear with their ears, lest they should understand with their hearts and turn, so that I should heal them'" (Matt. 13:14–15).

Romans 1:28 tells us, "And even as they did not like to retain God in their knowledge, God gave them over to a debased mind, to do those things which are not fitting."

Thus, it is God who lets us see the truth — lets us see that the evidence is all there — that He is Creator. However, in a very real sense, there has to be a willingness on our part to want to see as well. Why can the humanists, the evolutionists, not see that all the evidence supports exactly what the Bible says? It is because they do not want to see it. It is not because the evidence is not there. They refuse to allow the evidence to be correctly interpreted in the light of biblical teaching.

In Isaiah 50:10 we read, "Who among you fears the LORD? Who obeys the voice of His Servant? Who walks in darkness and has no light? Let him trust in the name of the LORD and rely upon his God."

Here is an analogy to help us understand. In John 11, we read that Jesus came to the tomb of Lazarus. Lazarus was dead. Remember, non-Christians are dead in trespasses and sin (Eph. 2:5). We could describe non-Christians as the walking dead.

Jesus first stated, "Take away the stone" (John 11:39). Now Jesus could have rolled that stone away (or made it disappear) with one word, but what humans could do, He got them to do. They rolled away the stone. But what humans could not do, Jesus did: "Lazarus, come forth!" (John 11:43) Jesus raised the dead.

I like to use the analogy that the act of rolling the stone away is akin to us as humans using observational science to do our best to convince the evolutionists that the evidence confirms the Bible's history. We answer questions and defend the Christian faith. But our arguments cannot raise the walking dead. So we make sure that as we argue (just as Paul would argue and confute), we point people to the *Word* of God and ensure we preach the Word and they hear the gospel. Then we pray that God will raise the dead.

It is my prayer that those who oppose the Creator God will come to trust in Him as Lord and Savior. When we read the rest of Isaiah 50, it should make each of us pray more for humanists and evolutionists who want to walk in their own light — in the light of man: "Look, all you who kindle a fire, who encircle yourselves with sparks: Walk in the light of your fire and in the sparks you have kindled — this you shall have from My hand: You shall lie down in torment" (Isa. 50:11).

We do not want this to be the fate of any human being. As the Lord says in His Word, it is not His desire that any should perish (2 Peter 3:9). However, God (who is a God of love) is also the God who is judge, and He cannot look upon sin (Hab. 1:13). Therefore, sin

must be judged for what it is. However, God in His infinite mercy sent His only begotten Son, "For God so loved the world that He gave His only begotten Son, that whoever believes in Him should not perish but have everlasting life" (John 3:16).

"In the beginning was the Word, and the Word was with God, and the Word was God. He was in the beginning with God. All things were made through Him, and without Him nothing was made that was made. In Him was life, and the life was the light of men" (John 1:1–4).

CHAPTER 5

CRUMBLING FOUNDATIONS

MILLIONS OF YEARS AND evolution have been popularized and presented as scientific truth, and many Christians have added millions of years and/or evolutionary belief to their biblical belief in God as Creator. Thus, while many Christians acknowledge that God created, they believe in evolution and/or millions of years. In fact, there are many different positions of compromise on Genesis within the Church and Christian academia, all with one thing in common: they attempt to add millions of years into God's Word. Such positions include the gap theory, theistic evolution, progressive creation, the framework hypothesis, the day-age view, the temple inauguration view, and many others. (See appendix 3 for more about other interpretations of Genesis.)

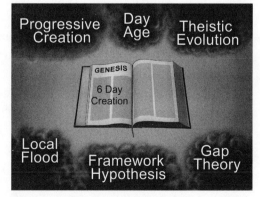

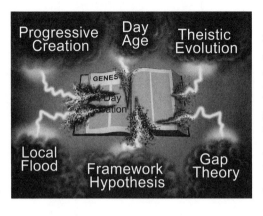

Widespread confusion has resulted, causing many in the Church (and particularly among younger generations) to question the plain statements of the Bible. Christians are no longer sure of what is truth and what is not in regard to the Genesis account of origins. Too many Christians have not realized the foundational importance of the creation/evolution/age of the earth issues. Ultimately, it is an authority issue. Who is the ultimate authority — man or God?

As already indicated, there is a connection between origins and issues affecting society such as marriage, abortion, sexual deviancy, parental authority, and so on. Now, as will become plain, I am not blaming belief in evolution and/or millions of years for such moral issues in the culture. However, the more generations are led to believe that the Bible's account of history in Genesis is not true, and the more they are taught that man's beliefs should be used to reinterpret the clear statements in the Bible concerning origins, then the more such people will also reinterpret the morality of the Bible on the basis of man's ideas. We are seeing that happen even now as more and more people in the Church take man's ideas in regard to marriage and attempt to justify gay marriage as legitimate.

How do we know what our beliefs should be in relation to these matters? Christians need to look deeply into the reasons why they believe as they do.

To begin to understand this, we must first consider the relevance of the creation account in Genesis. In John 5:46–47 we read of Jesus's words, "For if you believed Moses, you would believe Me; for he wrote about Me. But if you do not believe his writings, how will you believe My words?" Then in Luke, Jesus, speaking in a parable, quotes Abraham as saying, "If they do not hear Moses and the prophets, neither will they be persuaded though one rise from the dead" (Luke 16:31).

Both references underline the paramount importance placed on the writings of Moses, beginning with Genesis. In Luke 24:44, Jesus referred to the "Law of Moses" in an obvious reference to the five books of the Law (the Pentateuch), which includes Genesis, accepting Moses as author/compiler. In Acts 28:23 we read that Paul, in Rome, preached unto them Jesus from Moses and the prophets. These are all references to the writings of Moses. And there is one book of Moses that is referred to more often in the rest of the Bible than any other book: Genesis. But in theological and Bible colleges, in Christian and non-Christian circles, which book of the Bible is often the most attacked, mocked, scoffed at, thrown out, allegorized, and mythologized? Based on years of experience and research, I suggest it is the book of Genesis! The very writings that are quoted from more than any others in the Scriptures are the ones most attacked, disbelieved, or ignored. Why is that so?

Foundations under Attack

Psalm 11:3 asks, "If the foundations are destroyed, what can the righteous do?" It is important to understand the relationship the Psalmist is making. Society depends on moral foundations. By a mutual agreement that has sometimes been called a social contract, man, in an ordered and civilized society, sets limits to his own conduct. However, when such obligations are repudiated and the law collapses, along with the order it brings, what option has the man who seeks peace? The Psalmist is looking at the fact that whenever the foundations of society are undermined, then what have good and righteous men done to prevent its impending collapse?

For instance, if the foundation of a building collapses, the whole building will collapse. We see the collapse of the Christianized West before our very eyes in the 21st century. Why is the once very Christianized structure collapsing? Because a foundation has been attacked. Which foundation? The foundation of the authority of the Word of God.

Some quite correctly quoted Scriptures in saying that Jesus Christ is the foundation and He cannot be destroyed. In the context in which this verse from Psalm 11 is used, we are talking about the foundational knowledge upon which our moral framework is built. The foundational knowledge of Jesus Christ as Creator can be removed in people's thinking, whether they are from Australia, America, England, or any other society. This action does not mean Jesus Christ is not Creator, and neither does it mean that He has been dethroned. However, it does mean that in those nations that abandon this foundational basis, the whole fabric of society will suffer the consequences.

Again I quote from the Scriptures:

> In those days there was no king in Israel; everyone did what was right in his own eyes (Judg. 17:6).

If you destroy the foundations of anything, the structure will collapse. If you want to destroy any building, you are guaranteed early success if you destroy the foundations.

Likewise, if one wants to destroy Christianity, then one should destroy the foundational history given in the book of Genesis. Is it any wonder that Satan is attacking Genesis more than any other book?

The biblical doctrine of origins, as contained in the Book of Genesis, is foundational to all other doctrines of Scripture. If you refute or undermine in any way the biblical doctrine of origins, the rest of the Bible will be compromised. *Every single biblical doctrine of theology, directly or indirectly, ultimately has its basis in the Book of Genesis.*

Therefore, if you do not have a believing understanding of that book, you cannot hope to attain full comprehension of what Christianity is all about. If we want to understand the meaning of anything, we must understand its origins — its basis.

Genesis is the only book that provides an account of the origin of all the basic entities of life and the universe: the origin of life, of man, of government, of marriage, of culture, of nations, of death, of the chosen people, of sin, of diet and

clothes, of the solar system . . . the list is almost endless. The meaning of all these things is dependent on their origin. In the same way, the meaning and purpose of the Christian gospel depends on the origin of the problem for which the Savior's death was, and is, the solution. The history in Genesis 1–3 is foundational to an understanding of the gospel of Jesus Christ. It is there where we read of the origin of sin and man's need for a Savior. The very first time the gospel is preached is in Genesis 3:15:

> And I will put enmity between you and the woman, And between your seed and her Seed; He shall bruise your head, And you shall bruise His heel.

How would you answer the following questions? Imagine someone coming up to you and saying, "Hey, Christian, do you believe in marriage? Do you believe it means one man for one woman for life? If so, why?" Now, the average Christian would say that he or she believes in marriage because it is somewhere in the Bible, Paul said something about it, that adultery is sin, and there are some laws laid down about it.

If you are not a Christian, consider these questions: Are you married? Why? Why not just live with someone without bothering to marry? Do you believe marriage is one man for one woman for life? Why not six wives? Or six husbands?

What would happen if your son came home and said, "Dad, I am going to marry Bill tomorrow"? Sadly, such is becoming more commonplace these days.

You would likely say, "You can't do that, son! It's just not done!"

What if your son replied, "Yes it is, Dad. There are even churches that will marry us"? If you were *not* a Christian, what would you say to your son? Can you have any basis, any justification, for insisting that he should not live a homosexual lifestyle if he wants to?

When attempting to justify why they do or do not have a particular belief, many people today often have *opinions* rather than *reasons*. It is sometimes interesting to watch interviews on television news programs. I recall one program on Australian television years ago in which people were interviewed and asked to express their opinions concerning a government department's ruling to grant homosexual couples benefits similar to those received by married heterosexual couples. Some of the opinions expressed went like this: "It's not right." "It goes against my grain." "It's wrong." "It's not normal." "It's bad." "It shouldn't happen." "It's not good." "It shouldn't be allowed." "Why shouldn't they?" "People can do what they like!" Many other similar expressions were stated. But because such statements are only *opinions*, and thus subjective, we have seen the change that has occurred in the culture as gay marriage and the homosexual lifestyle have become more and more accepted by the culture as a whole throughout our Western world.

The change caused by following opinions in regard to the homosexual lifestyle is very evident in American culture. More and more states are embracing gay marriage and passing laws that are favorable to it. But this sort of thinking has also infiltrated the Church as some Christians have tried to argue based simply on opinions rather than on the absolute authority of Scripture.

A pastor of a major denominational church wrote a book recently called *What's the Least I Can Believe and Still Be a Christian?* The title alone reveals much about the content of the book — essentially, the author argues that major issues such as homosexual behavior are not clearly addressed in Scripture and so become matters of man's opinion. The author's position on homosexual behavior is ambiguous. While he says his church's position is "non-affirming," he says that is because "it is not yet ready to affirm homosexual behavior."[1] The author follows up this statement by writing, "We're still talking about it and debating it. We're still studying it and praying about it. So maybe one day our position will change. But for now this is where most of us stand."[2]

Despite the fact that God's Word is clear on the issue of homosexual behavior, this pastor has chosen to make his starting point man's *opinions* instead — and look at the fruit of such thinking! He and his congregation are debating and talking about the possibility of affirming homosexual behavior because they have the wrong starting point. Basically, whether they realize it or not, they are attempting to write their own rules for life.

---

1. Martin Thielen, *What's the Least I Can Believe and Still Be a Christian?: A Guide to What Matters Most* (Louisville, KY: Westminster John Knox Press, 2011), p. 56.
2. Ibid., p. 58.

Once, after I had spoken on creation and evolution at one public school, a student said to me, "I want to write my own rules about life and decide what I want to do."

I said, "You can do that if you like, son, but in that case, why can't I shoot you?"

He replied, "You can't do that!"

"Why not?"

"Because it's not right," he said.

I said to him, "Why is it not right?"

"Because it is wrong."

"Why is it wrong?"

He looked perplexed and said to me, "Because it is not right!"

This student had a problem. On what basis could he decide something was right or wrong? He had started the conversation by indicating he wanted to write his own rules. He was told that if he wanted to write his own rules, then surely I could write my rules. He certainly agreed with this. If that was so, and I could convince enough people to agree with me that characters like him were dangerous, then why should we not eliminate him from society? He started to insist again, "It's not right — it's wrong — it's not right." If he had no basis on an absolute authority that sets the rules, it was really a battle of his opinion versus my opinion. Perhaps the strongest or the cleverest would win. He got the point.

Some people have the opinion that a homosexual lifestyle is wrong. However, if it is just an opinion, then surely the view that homosexuality is acceptable is just as valid as any other view. And where does it stop? What about euthanasia, bestiality, or pedophilia? Who decides what is right or wrong? The point is, it is not a matter of one's opinion. It is really a matter of what the One who is Creator, who owns us, gives us as a basis for the principles governing this area of life. What does God say in His Word concerning these issues?

Christians have standards of right and wrong because they accept that there is a Creator, and that as Creator, He has direct ownership over His creation. He owns us not only because He created us but also because the Scriptures say, "Or do you not know that . . . you are not your own? For you were bought at a price" (1 Cor. 6:19–20). God created everything; therefore, He has absolute authority. Because humans are created beings, they are under total obligation to the One who has absolute authority over them. Our absolute authority has the right to set the rules. It is in our own best interest to obey because He is Creator. Thus, what is right and what is wrong is not a matter of anyone's opinion but must be in accord with the principles found in the Word of God, who has authority over us. Just as a car designer provides a manual for correct maintenance of what he has designed and made, so too does our Creator supply His creation with all the instructions necessary to live a full, free, and abundant life. God has provided His set of instructions not out of some spiteful or killjoy design but because He loves us and knows what is best for us.

Structures without Foundations

We often hear comments from parents that their children have rebelled against the Christian ethic, asking why they should obey their parents' rules. One major reason for this is that many Christian parents have not instructed their children from foundational perspectives concerning what they should or should not do. If children see rules as no more than their parents' opinions, then why should they obey them? It does make an enormous difference when children are taught from the earliest age that God is Creator and that He has determined what is right and wrong. The rules come from God, and therefore, they must be obeyed. It is impossible to build any structure without a foundation, but that is what many parents are trying to do in the training of their children. The results of such attempts are all around us — a generation with increasing numbers rejecting God and the absolutes of Christianity.

Another major issue that was highlighted as a result of the *Already Gone* research is that, because so many Christian leaders and parents have told kids they can believe in evolution and/or millions of years, biblical authority has been undermined.[3] After all, if generations are told they can reinterpret Genesis on the basis of what secularists say about the age of the earth and evolutionary ideas, why should they not also reinterpret what the Bible teaches about marriage and

---

3. Ken Ham and Britt Beemer, *Already Gone: Why Your Kids Will Quit the Church and What You Can Do to Stop It*, with Todd Hillard (Green Forest, AR: Master Books, 2009).

other issues on the basis of what the same secularists believe? This is what has been happening. Because of compromise in the Church, increasing numbers of the next generation have made man the authority — not God.

At one church, a very sad father came to me and said, "My sons rebelled against Christianity. I remember their coming to me and saying, 'Why should we obey *your* rules?' I had never thought to tell them that they weren't my rules. I only realized this morning how I should have given them the foundations of God as Creator and explained that He sets the rules. I have the responsibility before Him as head of my house to see that they are carried through. They only saw the Christian doctrines I was conveying to them as my opinions or the Church's opinions. Now they won't have anything to do with the Church. They are doing what is right in their own eyes — not God's."

This is so typical of today's Christian society, and it is very much related to this issue of foundations. Many parents do not realize they are not laying the proper foundation at home by placing the emphasis on God as Creator and by taking God at His Word in Genesis. When their children go to school, they are given another foundation: God is not Creator, and we are simply products of evolutionary processes over millions of years. And sadly, many parents (and pastors) tell these same kids they can believe the evolutionary ideas they are taught at school — as long as they believe God did it!

The problem, however, is that it is not what God said He did. When these same children compare evolutionary ideas with the Bible, they begin to increasingly doubt they can trust the Bible in anything it says. No wonder so many children rebel. One cannot build a house from the roof down. We must start from the foundation and build upon this. Sadly, many parents have built a structure for the next generation that does not have the foundational understanding that Jesus Christ is the Creator and His Word is true from the beginning. They are not teaching their children that they need to judge man's fallible ideas about the past on the basis of the Word of God.

Students in most of our schools are given a totally anti-biblical foundation: the foundation of evolution and millions of years.

This foundation, of course, will ultimately not allow the Christian structure to stand. A structure of a different type — secular humanism and its relative morality — is the one built on this foreign foundation.

Many parents have said it was when their children went to high school or college that they drifted away from Christianity. Many of their children rejected Christianity entirely. If there was never an emphasis on constructing the right foundation at home, it is little wonder the Christian structure collapsed.

The *Already Gone* research, published in 2009, was conducted to find out why in America two-thirds of young people now leave the Church by college age.[4] It has thrown much light on what has been happening. This research showed clearly that these young people who walk away from the Church begin doubting the Bible at a young age. About 40 percent doubt the Bible by the end of middle school (grades 7–9), and an additional 45 percent doubt the Bible by the end of high school. Around 90 percent of these kids attend public schools. We are losing the coming generations at a young age. The research also showed that those who teach these kids in church and in the home are undermining their understanding of the authority of God's Word with evolution and millions of years. It was also obvious that generations of kids are not being taught how to defend the Christian faith because they are not being taught how to answer the skeptical questions of the age. There is a great lack of training in apologetics from both the church and the home.

Regrettably, in my experience I have found that many Christian schools and Christian colleges/seminaries also teach evolution and/ or millions of years, so parents should not assume that their children are necessarily safe because they attend a Christian school. The school may claim that it teaches creation, but on a detailed investigation, it is often found that they teach that God used evolution and/or millions of years in creation.

In 2010, Answers in Genesis contracted with America's Research Group (who also conducted the *Already Gone* research) to conduct research into what Christian colleges are teaching. This research was

---

4. Ibid., p. 21.

published in 2011 in *Already Compromised*. The results are disturbing. I would encourage every parent and every student contemplating attending a Christian college to read this book.

This same problem of a structure without a foundation is also reflected in another way. Many Christians may be against abortion, sexual deviancy, and other moral problems in society, yet they cannot give proper justification for their opposition. Most Christians have an idea of what is wrong and what is right, but they do not understand why. And others view Christians' lack of reasons for their positions as just opinion. And why should our opinion be any more valid than that of someone else?

Another problem today is that many Christians think they should argue from what they perceive is a neutral position. They have been indoctrinated to believe that if they use the Bible in such arguments, then they are imposing their religion on people! However, if they do not use the Bible, then, as discussed in preceding chapters, there is only one other starting point — the word of man! Thus, in reality they have lost the debate before they started because they are now only arguing from a subjective perspective. As I have stated previously, there is no neutral position because man is not neutral:

> He who is not with Me is against Me, and he who does not gather with Me scatters abroad (Matt. 12:30).

> Then Jesus spoke to them again, saying, "I am the light of the world. He who follows Me shall not walk in darkness, but have the light of life" (John 8:12).

> . . . the imagination of man's heart is evil from his youth (Gen. 8:21).

> As it is written: "There is none righteous, no, not one; there is none who understands; there is none who seeks after God" (Rom. 3:10–11).

> For this they willfully forget: that by the word of God the heavens were of old, and the earth standing out of water and in the water, by which the world that then existed perished, being flooded with water (2 Pet. 3:5–6).

Building on the True Foundation

All these issues relate to an understanding of what the Bible is all about. It is not just a guidebook for life. It is the very basis (starting point) upon which all of our thinking must be built. Unless we understand that book, we will *not* have a proper understanding of God and His relationship to man and thus of what a Christian worldview is all about. That is why Jesus said in John 5:47 that we must believe the writings of Moses.

For instance, to understand why living a homosexual lifestyle is wrong, one has to understand that the basis for marriage comes from Genesis. It is in Genesis where we read that God ordained marriage and declared it to be one man for one woman for life. God created Adam and Eve — not two men or two women. He created a male and a female for the first marriage.

When Jesus was asked about marriage in Matthew 19, He quoted from Genesis 1 and 2 to remind everyone that marriage is to be between a male and a female:

> And He answered and said to them, "Have you not read that He who made them at the beginning 'made them male and female,' and said, 'For this reason a man shall leave his father and mother and be joined to his wife, and the two shall become one flesh'? So then, they are no longer two but one flesh. Therefore what God has joined together, let not man separate" (Matt. 19:4–6).

Also, one primary importance for marriage, as stated in Malachi 2:15, is that God created two to be "one" so that they could produce "godly offspring":

> But did He not make them one, Having a remnant of the Spirit? And why one? He seeks godly offspring. Therefore take heed to your spirit, And let none deal treacherously with the wife of his youth.

In response to the marriage problems of the day, the prophet is making a reference to "one flesh" in Genesis 2 when he asks the question concerning the meaning of marriage. Why did God make two one (one flesh)? Why marriage? And the answer is clear: to produce not just offspring but godly offspring. The point is that this reference to the meaning of marriage also makes it clear that marriage is between a man and a woman! Anything else destroys what God ordained for marriage and the family.

In fact, the family is the first and most fundamental of all human institutions God ordained in Scripture. The family is the educational unit of the nation. The family is to produce godly offspring who will influence the world for Christ and who will then produce godly offspring who will influence the world for Christ, generation after generation. Gay marriage destroys this and runs totally against what our Creator determined marriage is to be.

When one understands that there are specific roles God ordained for men and women, one has reasons for standing against any legislation that weakens or destroys the family. Thus, a homosexual lifestyle is anti-God, and so it is wrong — not because it is our opinion but because God, the absolute authority, says so. (Note particularly Lev. 18:22; Rom. 1:24, 26–27; and Gen. 2:23–24.)

We must reinforce in our own thinking, and in our Christian churches, that the Bible *is* the Word of God and that God has absolute authority over our lives. We must listen to what He says in relation to the principles to live by in *every area* of life, *regardless of what anyone's opinion is.* A human-based, opinion-oriented style of argument permeates the Church in many ways. Consider the issue of abortion.

I have been to Bible studies where groups are discussing abortion. Many of the members give their opinion about what they think, but they give no reference to the Bible. They say such things as "what if their daughter were raped," or "if the baby were going to be deformed," or "if somebody wouldn't be able to cope with looking after the child," then perhaps abortion would be acceptable. This is where our churches are falling down in their responsibilities. The idea that everyone can have an opinion devoid of a basis in biblical principles has crept into our churches and is one of the main reasons why we have so many problems sorting out doctrine and determining what we should believe. It is not a matter of autonomous human opinion about what is developing in a mother's womb; it is a matter of what God says in His Word concerning the principles that must govern our thinking. Psalm 139, Psalm 51, Jeremiah 1, and many other passages of Scripture make it quite plain that, at the point of conception, we are human beings. Therefore, abortion in all instances must be viewed as killing a human being. That is the only way of looking at the matter. It is time we woke up. When it comes to such issues, we must take God's view, not man's!

But in a church culture where man's opinions about origins are being used to reinterpret God's Word, we should not be surprised that such an opinion-oriented philosophy (putting one's trust in man's word instead of God's Word) permeates people's thinking.

If God's people stood on the authority of His Word like they should, many of the problems we have in churches today would obviously be more easily solved. A large conference of one particular Protestant denomination was discussing whether the church should ordain women as pastors. It was interesting to see what happened. Someone jumped to his feet and said, "We should ordain women as pastors because they are just as bright as men." Another commented that we have women doctors and women lawyers, so why should we not also have women pastors? Somebody else said women are equal to men and therefore should be pastors. But at this and other such conferences, how many people do we hear stating, "God made man; God made woman. He has given them their special roles in this world. The only way we could ever attempt to come to the right conclusion about this issue is to start from what He says concerning the roles of men and women." The trouble is, everyone wants to have his or her own opinion without reference to God's authoritative Word.

At one meeting, a lady responded in a rather irate tone to what I had said about the roles of men and women. She said that she should not be submissive to her husband until he was as perfect as Christ.

I then asked her where this was stated in the Bible. She said it was obvious the Bible taught this. Therefore, she did not have to be in submission to her husband. I repeated my question to her, insisting that she show me where in the Bible it made such a statement or gave a principle whereby one could come to that conclusion logically. She could not show me, but she still insisted that if her husband could not be as perfect as Christ, she did not have to be submissive to him. It was obvious to everyone present that she wanted her own opinion regardless of what the Scripture stated. She did not want to be submissive to her husband, and she did not want to obey the Scriptures.

Another place where we often hear people's opinions expressed in all sorts of ways is at members' meetings in churches. I have been at meetings where they were electing deacons. Someone would suggest a certain person to be a deacon because he was such a good man. When somebody else suggested that the qualifications for a deacon as given in the Scriptures should be applied, some objected, saying that they could not rule out a person from being a deacon just because he did not measure up to the qualifications given in Scripture. In other words, people's opinions, according to some, were above Scripture.

There are many ways in which we see this man-centered philosophy permeating our Christian society. The principal of a Christian school was telling me that he has a number of parents who object to his strict discipline, which is based upon biblical principles. Their objections usually took the form of comparison with other schools or of reasoning that their children were not as bad as other children around the neighborhood. Instead of comparing the standards with God's Word, they compared them with other people.

For instance, some parents insisted that because there were other students in the school who had not been caught doing wrong things, their own children should not be punished. The principal pointed out that if this were applied in society, enormous problems would result. For example, does this mean that police should not prosecute a driver they happen to catch with a high alcohol content in his blood just because many other drivers who also have a high alcohol content were not caught? These parents were upset because of the standard the principal applied — a standard based upon the authority of God's Word.

Paul says, "Therefore, brethren, stand fast and hold the traditions which you were taught, whether by word or our epistle" (2 Thess. 2:15). Do we stand fast, or do we waver? What we are seeing in our society is an outward expression, in more and more of its naked ferocity, of the rejection of God and His absolutes, and the growing belief that only human opinions matter. Sadly, this is not surprising in such an age where man's opinions concerning origins (evolution and/ or millions of years) are being accepted over God's Word in Genesis — and this acceptance permeates the Church and Christian homes.

The reason for much of the conflict throughout the Church at the present time is that people are fighting over their opinions. It is not a matter of opinion, yours or mine. It is what *God* says that matters. The basis for our thinking should be the principles from His Word. They must determine our actions.

To understand this, we must also appreciate that Genesis 1–11 is foundational to the entire Christian philosophy. But many people in our churches today do not trust Genesis. Consequently, they (particularly the coming generations) do not know what else in the Bible to trust. They treat the Bible as an interesting book containing some vague sort of religious truth. This view is destroying the Church and our society, and it is time religious leaders wake up to that fact. Not to take Genesis 1 through 11 literally is to do violence to the rest of Scripture.

As the late James Barr, a renowned Hebrew scholar and professor, said in a personal letter dated April 23, 1984, "So far as I know, there is no professor of Hebrew or Old Testament at any world-class university who does not believe that the writer(s) of Genesis 1 through 11 intended to convey to their readers the ideas that (a) creation took place in a series of six days which were the same as the days of 24 hours we now experience; (b) the figures contained in the Genesis genealogies provided by simple addition a chronology from the beginning of the world up to later stages in the biblical story; (c) Noah's flood was understood to be worldwide and extinguished all human and animal life except for those in the ark."[5]

---

5. Douglas F. Kelly, *Creation and Change: Genesis 1:1–2:4 in the Light of Changing Scientific Paradigms* (Great Britain: Christian Focus Publications, 1997), p. 50–51.

Please note that many, if not most of these world-class scholars do not believe in the Bible or Christianity anyway, so they are not interested in wresting the Scriptures to somehow try to make their religion fit with evolution. Disbelieve it if you wish, but it is impossible to make out that Genesis is saying anything other than what it says. We can see now that those who say that the clear teaching of Genesis is not what it actually means are not doing so on the basis of literary or linguistic scholarship but because of partial surrender to the pressure of evolutionary/millions of years thinking. In actual fact, they are making man the starting point and his opinion the foundation — not God and His Word.

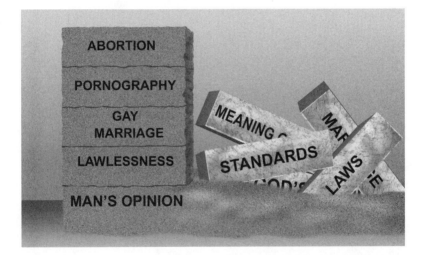

Chapter 6

GENESIS DOES MATTER

LET US LOOK IN DETAIL at some important Christian doctrines to show why this emphasis on a literal Genesis must be accepted. Suppose that we are being questioned concerning the doctrines Christians believe. Think carefully how you would answer in detail.

- Why do we believe in marriage — and why strictly between a man and a woman?

- Why do we promote the wearing of clothes?

- Why are there rules — right and wrong?

- Why are we sinners? What does that mean?

- Why is there death and suffering in the world?

- Why is there to be a new heaven and a new earth?

We will consider each doctrine carefully because it is important to have reasons for what we believe. In fact, God expects His children to be ready to give answers — to give reasons for what they believe. In 1 Peter 3:15 we read, "But sanctify the Lord God in your hearts, and always be ready to give a defense to everyone who asks you a reason for the hope that is in you, with meekness and fear."

Christianity, as distinct from atheism, is not a blind faith but an objective one; our object is Jesus Christ. He does reveal Himself to those who come by faith, believing that He is. John 14:21 says, "And I will love him and manifest Myself to him." Hebrews 11:6 says, "For he who comes to God must believe that He is, and that He is a rewarder of those who diligently seek Him."

If reasons for the validity of the Christian's faith are not forthcoming, his witness is weakened and open to ridicule. Christians must be prepared to make an intelligent defense of the gospel by arming themselves with knowledge and an understanding of the forms unbelief takes in these days. In 1 Peter 3:15, the word that is translated "defense" (and sometimes "answer") comes from the Greek word *apologia*. This word means to give a legal plea and so give a reasoned defense of the faith. Sadly, most Christians cannot do this. They cannot answer the skeptical questions of today that are directed at Christians as skeptics challenge the validity of the history in Genesis.

Most Christian homes and most churches (as well as most Christian academic institutions) do not teach children and adults how to answer these skeptical questions and thus prepare them for the attacks they will encounter. There is a sad lack of teaching apologetics in the Christian world. In *Already Gone*, details are given as to why two-thirds of young people are leaving the Church in America by the time they reach college age.[1] The lack of the teaching on apologetics greatly contributes to this problem. And because around 90 percent of kids from church homes go to public schools, these kids brought up in the church are being taught apologetics at school — but apologetics that undermine the Bible.

The minority of Christian teachers who are missionaries would agree that, by and large, the public education system has all but thrown God out and various curricula and textbooks teach students the supposed evidence for millions of years and other evolutionary ideas. Thus, most church kids are taught a defense of the secular

---

1. For more, see Ken Ham and Britt Beemer, *Already Gone: Why Your Kids Will Quit the Church and What You Can Do to Stop It*, with Todd Hillard (Green Forest, AR: Master Books, 2009).

worldview at school, but at church and at home, they are in most instances taught that the Bible is a book of stories.

The net result is a loss of the majority of the next generation from the Church and wishy-washy Christians who believe in many things but are not sure why. Personal witnessing can lose its impact if the Christian fails to share intelligent reasons for his faith. This must be avoided, lest ridicule and dishonor come to the name of Christ.

From my experience, most Christians today are intimidated by the world because they do not know how to answer questions challenging their faith and the truth of God's Word in today's increasingly secularized culture. This is one of the reasons why in our Western world, a small minority of atheists control the education systems, imposing their secular religion on the culture.

A good example of what happens when we do not give reasons for what we believe can be seen in a letter to the editor of an Arizona newspaper. It reads as follows:

> When I was a youngster, we all believed that men had one less rib than women because God created Eve with one of Adam's ribs. When the story was written five to ten thousand years later after Noah and the world flood, how many people could read, much less write? . . . You say you are a teacher of creationism in school classes. How would you answer these questions? If Noah took two of each animal on the ark, where did he get polar bears, bison, and kangaroos? You might answer that those animals lived in the Eastern Mediterranean area back then. The next question would be, how did the various colors of humans evolve from one white (deeply tanned) family in 5,000 or even 50,000 years? . . . When I was growing up in a deeply religious family, I was told not to question the Bible and other religious writings. I got no answer then, and 70 years later I am still waiting for a reasonable explanation.

This letter has so much incorrect information I realized it would take a great amount of time to talk through the many issues addressed. I personally spoke to the writer of this letter. As we talked, it became obvious that he had been told to accept the Bible by blind faith and was never given any useful answers. Omission caused him to reject evangelical Christianity. How sad! And the answers to these sorts of questions are available in the plethora of books and other resources readily available today.[2] So let us give reasons (a defense) for what we believe as we discuss the subjects mentioned above.

Marriage

When Jesus was asked questions concerning divorce in Matthew 19:4–5, He immediately referred to the origin, and thus the foundation, of marriage. He said, "Have you not read that He who made them at the beginning 'made them male and female,' and said, 'For this reason a man shall leave his father and mother and be joined to his wife, and the two shall become one flesh'?" And from where did Jesus quote? Genesis! Jesus was saying, "Don't you understand there is a historical basis for marriage?" If we did not have this historical basis, we would not have marriage. The only basis is in the Scriptures. You can say it is convenient for you, but  you cannot tell your son he cannot marry Bill or for that matter, Julie *and* Susan. Likewise, extramarital relationships would be a tolerable alternative. You would have no justification for thinking otherwise.

Now if we go back to Genesis, we read how God took dust and made a man. From the man's side, He made a woman. Adam's first recorded words were, "This is now bone of my bones and flesh of my flesh" (Gen. 2:23). They were one flesh. When a man and a woman marry, they become one. This is the historical basis. Also, a husband and wife are to cleave to one another as if they had no parents — just like Adam and Eve, who had no parents. We know it is to be a heterosexual relationship. Why? Because, as stated before, God made Adam and Eve (a man and a woman — *not* a man and a man). That is the only basis for marriage, and that is why we know that homosexual behavior is an evil, perverse, and unnatural deviation — and gay marriage is against what God clearly teaches in His Word.

---

2. For resources on the creation/evolution debate, apologetics, and more, visit the Answers in Genesis website and online store at www.AnswersinGenesis.org.

In 2012, President Barack Obama (USA) declared his support for gay marriage:

> I've always been adamant that gay and lesbian Americans should be treated fairly and equally. . . . It is important for me to go ahead and affirm that I think same-sex couples should be able to get married.[3]

What if someone were to tell President Obama that a true marriage is strictly between a man and a woman because God built the doctrine of marriage on the history of the creation of the first male and female in Genesis? Sadly, in this day and age, I would not be surprised if he were to respond with something like this: "Well, many Christian leaders and Christian academics tell me Genesis is not meant to be taken as literal history, so marriage can be defined in different ways."

It is time that the Church stopped compromising God's Word in Genesis and stood its ground against the increasing acceptance of homosexual behavior as something natural or normal or as an acceptable alternative. Paul would not have written about homosexuality in the way that he did in Romans if he did not have that historical basis. (Please note that although as Christians we condemn the sin of homosexual behavior, we are to be grace-oriented toward the homosexual and seek his or her deliverance from bondage.)

The gay marriage issue has become a major one in the early 21st century, and sadly, most of the Church does not deal with it in the correct way because the Church has so compromised the foundation of marriage as outlined in the Book of Genesis.

What about the rest of the Bible's teaching on marriage? There is another aspect, which has to do with the family. It is the reason many Christian families go to pieces or their offspring go astray. In the majority of Christian homes today, it is usually the mother who teaches the children spiritually. What an unfortunate thing it is that fathers have not embraced their God-given responsibility. When one looks at the biblical roles given to fathers and mothers, it is the fathers who are allocated the responsibility of providing for their

---

3. Barack Obama, interview by Robin Roberts, "Obama Affirms Support for Same-Sex Marriage," *ABC News Special Report*, ABC, May 9, 2012, http://abc-news.go.com/GMA/video/obama-sex-marriage-legal-16312904.

children and providing the family's spiritual and physical needs (Isa. 38:19; Prov. 1:8; Eph. 6:4). One result of this role reversal is that the sons often stop coming to church. Christian girls who have not been trained properly by their fathers concerning the marriage relationship often disobey the Lord by dating and marrying non-Christian men.

A young woman approached me and said she was married to a non-Christian. She explained that when she was dating this man, she compared him to her father and saw no real difference. Yet her father was a Christian. But because her father was not the spiritual head of the house, she did not see any real difference between him and the person she was dating. She saw no reason to make sure that her husband-to-be was a Christian. Now that she is married and has children, there are some extreme problems with their marriage regarding the bringing up of their children.

A major reason for so many of the problems in Christian families today is that fathers have not taken their God-commanded responsibility of being priests in their household. As a husband and a father, he is also a priest to his wife and children. It is not, however, a boss relationship where men despotically lord their headship over women. Many secular feminists think the Bible teaches a tyrannical relationship in marriage. Unfortunately, because of the influence of feminism in the Church, many Christians who call themselves evangelical feminists claim the Bible does not affirm male headship at all. However, the Bible does teach that husbands are to be godly heads of their families. But anyone who uses these biblical role absolutes to justify one person's seeking power over another has completely missed the whole message of Jesus Christ (Eph. 5:22–33; John 13:5). The Bible also says we are to submit one to another (Eph. 5:21). If you do not adopt the God-given roles set out in Scripture, you will find that your family will not function as God intended, and problems usually follow. The Bible also tells husbands to love their wives as Christ loved the Church (Eph. 5:25). In many instances, if husbands loved their wives this way, it would make it easier for many women to be submissive to them.[4]

---

4. For more about the biblical principles for the roles of men and women in marriage and how to raise godly offspring in an ungodly world, see Ken Ham and Steve Ham, *Raising Godly Children in an Ungodly World: Leaving a Lasting Legacy*, Todd Hillard, editor (Green Forest, AR: Master Books, 2006).

Why Clothes?

Consider why we wear clothes. Is it to keep warm? What if we lived in the tropics? Is it to look nice? If these are our only reasons, why wear clothes? Why not take them off when we want to, where we want to? Does it really matter if one goes nude publicly? Ultimately, the only reason for insisting that clothes must be worn is a moral one. If there is a moral reason, it must have a basis somewhere; therefore, there must be standards connected to the moral reason. What then are the standards? Many in our culture (including Christians) just ac-

cept the fashions of the day. Parents, what about the training of your children? What do you say to them about clothes?

In her paper "Greek Clothing Regulations: Sacred and Profane," Harrianne Mills had this to say: "Since the demise, roughly one hundred years ago, of the biblically based theory that clothes are worn because of modesty, various theories have been put forward by anthropologists concerned with the origins and functions of clothing."[5]

Why do we wear clothes? There is a moral basis if you go back to the Scriptures. We read in Genesis that when God made Adam and Eve, they were naked. But sin came into the world, and sin distorts everything. Sin distorts nakedness. Immediately Adam and Eve knew they were naked, and they tried to make coverings out of fig leaves. God came to their rescue, providing garments by killing an animal. This was the first blood sacrifice; it was a covering for their sin.

On a deeper level, God was really telling Adam and Eve that there would be a solution to the sin problem — a solution in one to come, who would be the ultimate sacrifice. The Israelites had to sacrifice animals over and over again, because as Hebrews 10:4 states, "For it is not possible that the blood of bulls and goats could take away sins." Humans are not connected to the animals; humans were made in

---

5. Harrianne Mills, "Greek Clothing Regulations: Sacred and Profane," *Zeit schrift fur Papyrologie und Epigraphie*, Band 55, 1984.

the image of God. An animal sacrifice cannot solve the sin problem; it can only point to the fact that one day there would be one who would die "once for all" (Heb. 10:10). Clothing is a reminder of our sin problem and the fact that the first sacrifice only covered our sin. It could not take our sin away. The only one who can take away our sin is our resurrected Savior, the Lord Jesus Christ.

Additionally, men are very easily sexually aroused. That is why semi-naked women are used in television and magazine advertisements. Parents need to explain to their daughters how easily a woman's body can sexually arouse a man. They need to know because many of them do not understand what happens to a man. At one church, after I had spoken on the topic of clothing, a young woman came up and told me that she had only been a Christian for six months. She was dating a young Christian man and was perplexed as to why he often told her not to wear certain things. Every time she asked him why, he started to feel embarrassed. She had not realized before that what she wore (or did not wear) could put a stumbling block in a man's way by causing him to commit adultery in his heart.

Fathers need to explain to their daughters how men react to a woman's body. They also need to explain to their sons that although women's clothes, or lack of them, can be a stumbling block to males, it is not an excuse for them in relation to what their minds do with what they see. Job had an answer for this problem: "I have made a covenant with my eyes; Why then should I look upon a young woman?" (Job 31:1). As Christians, males should have a covenant with their eyes and be reminded of this when lustful thoughts come as a result of what they see or hear.

Jesus stated that if a man lusts after a woman in his heart, he commits adultery in his heart: "But I say to you that whoever looks at a woman to lust for her has already committed adultery with her in his heart" (Matt. 5:28). Sin distorts nakedness. Even the perfect relationship experienced by Adam and Eve before the Fall degenerated. After the Fall, they hid from God and were ashamed of their nakedness. Many Christian women wear clothes that really accentuate their sexuality. And many a roving eye follows every movement. But what is happening? Men are committing adultery in their hearts — adultery for which they and the women will have to answer.

In many Christian homes, parents have certain beliefs about clothing. They say to their teenagers, "You can't wear that."

The teenagers reply, "But why not?"

"Because it is not the Christian thing," answer the parents.

"Why not?" ask the teenagers again.

"Because Christians don't wear that," the parents insist.

"Why not?" the reply comes.

Then you often hear daughters saying, "You're old-fashioned, Mom and Dad." They are saying that their parents have one opinion, but they have another opinion. For the most part, children are going to stick with their own opinions. However, it is not a matter of the parents' opinion or the child's opinion. In order for the parents to save face, they often resort to an imposed legalism. What a difference it makes when parents use Genesis as a basis to explain to their children why they must do this or that with regard to clothing, particularly if they have already solidly trained their children that God is Creator, that He sets the rules, and that Genesis is foundational to all doctrine. It is infinitely better than parents saying, "This is what you *will* do," and imposing this standard on their children with no basis. However, as we read in Ephesians 6:1, "Children, obey your parents in the Lord, for this is right." Children must obey their parents, and that is not a matter of their opinion, either.

Certainly, fashions change, and culturally, we will want to keep up with such changes. However, at the same time we need to always remember that there is a moral basis for wearing clothes because of what sin has done to nakedness. We must understand how men are created. Man was designed to be easily aroused sexually and to respond to one woman (his wife). This was, and is, necessary for procreation in marriage. However, sin distorts this, and it is wrong for a man to look lustfully on any woman other than his wife. Therefore, clothing should minimize to the greatest extent any stumbling block laid in a man's way. But a man is no less guilty if he succumbs to the second look. One should not simply accept the fashions of the day without understanding there is a moral basis for clothing; therefore, there are standards. Knowing what men are like and knowing what sin does to nakedness, we thus have a basis for understanding what the standards should be.

Why Law and Morality?

What do you tell your children about laws? Perhaps you tell them some things are right and some are wrong, but do you ever explain to them the origin of right and wrong? Would you say we have right and wrong because God has given us laws? If so, why is that? Why does He have a right to say what is right and what is wrong?

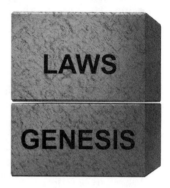

Why is there right and wrong (e.g., the Ten Commandments)? Remember the story in Matthew 19:16–17 when the man came to Jesus and said to Him: "'Good Teacher, what good thing shall I do that I may have eternal life?' So He said to him, 'Why do you call Me good? No one is good but One, that is, God.'" How do you decide if something is right or wrong or good or bad? God, the only One who is good, created us and therefore owns us. Thus, we are obligated to Him, and we must obey Him. He has the right to set the rules. He knows everything there is to know about everything (i.e., He has absolute knowledge), and therefore we must obey. That is why we have absolutes, why there are standards, and why there is right and wrong.

Now, if you are *not* a Christian and you think some things are right and some are wrong, why do you think like that? You have no basis for such a decision. How do you arrive at your standards? How do you decide what is good and bad? Most non-Christians who believe there is a right and wrong are practicing the Christian ethic.

Atheistic evolutionary philosophy says, "There is no God. All is the result of chance and randomness. Death and struggle are the order of the day, not only now but indefinitely into the past and future." If this is true, there is no basis for right and wrong. The more people believe in evolution and millions of years, the more they are going to say, "There is no God. Why should I obey authority? Why should there be rules against aberrant sexual behavior? Why should there be rules concerning abortion? After all, evolution tells us we are all animals. So killing babies by abortion is no worse than chopping the head off a fish or a chicken." *It does matter whether you believe in evolution or creation! It affects every area of your life.*

"For by the law is the knowledge of sin" (Romans 3:20)

This issue comes down to the simple fact explained by Paul in Romans 3:20, "For by the law is the knowledge of sin." In Romans 7:7 he continues, "I would not have known sin except through the law."

The existence of God is nowhere defended by Scripture. This fact is taken as being obvious. Who He is and what He has done is clearly explained. Neither is there any doubt as to His sovereign authority over His creation or what our attitude should be toward Him as Creator. He has the right to set the rules. We have the responsibility *to obey and rejoice in His goodness* or to disobey and suffer His judgment.

Adam, the first man, made this choice. He chose to rebel. Sin is rebellion against God and His will. Genesis tells us that this first act of human rebellion took place in the Garden of Eden.

To understand what sin is all about — that all humans are sinners — and how to recognize sin, God gave us the Law. He had the right and the loving concern to do this. He is Creator, and His character allows for no less. All powerful, all loving, all gracious, He has laid down for us the rules by which we must live if our lives are to develop in the way they should. As Paul concludes in Romans 7:7, "For I would not have known covetousness unless the law had said, 'You shall not covet.'"

The Bible clearly teaches that each human being is a sinner in a state of rebellion against God. Initially, the Law was given, as Paul states, to explain sin. But knowing about sin was not a solution to the problem. More was needed. The Creator had not forgotten His commitment to and love of His creation, for He set the payment and paid the price — *Himself.* God's Son, the Lord Jesus Christ, who is God, suffered the Curse of death on the Cross and became sin for us so that God could pour out His judgment upon sin. But just as all die in Adam, so all who believe in Christ's atoning death and Resurrection live in Him.

Those who oppose the Creator are opposing the One who is the absolute authority — the One who sets the rules and *keeps them.*

The Book of Judges states, "In those days there was no king in Israel; everyone did what was right in his own eyes" (Judges 17:6). People today are little different. They want evolution and millions of years taught as fact and the belief in creation banished because they, too, want to be a law unto themselves. They want to maintain the rebellious nature they have inherited from Adam, and they will *not* accept the authority of the One who, as Creator and lawgiver, has the right to tell them exactly what to do.

This really is what the creation/evolution/millions of years conflict is all about. Does God the Creator have the right to tell a person what he must do with his life? Or can man decide for himself what he wants to do without suffering the consequences? These are not rhetorical questions. Their very nature demands an answer from every individual. Thus, it comes down to whether or not man is autonomous and therefore can decide everything for himself or whether he is owned by God. Most want to be autonomous and believe they can act according to their own desires and understanding. But man is not autonomous, and there the battle rages.

The Bible tells us that those who trust in the Lord and are indwelt by His Holy Spirit will show the fruit of the Spirit: "love, joy, peace, longsuffering, kindness, goodness, faithfulness, gentleness, self-control" (Gal. 5:22–23). Those who are not indwelt by the Spirit of God and who reject the God of creation will reflect the fruit of this rejection: "adultery, fornication, uncleanness, lewdness, idolatry, sorcery, hatred, contentions, jealousies, outbursts of wrath, selfish ambitions, dissensions, heresies, envy, murders, drunkenness, revelries, and the like" (Gal. 5:19–21). The Bible states clearly that corrupt roots bring forth evil fruit. Pornography, abortion, homosexuality, lawlessness, euthanasia, infanticide, loose morals, unfaithfulness in marriage, and other such things — practices that are becoming more and more prevalent in today's society — are certainly fruit of corrupt roots. They are the corrupt roots of evolution firmly entrenched in the compost of humanistic thinking.

Evolution and its foundation of millions of years is an anti-God religion held by many people today as justification for their continued pursuit of self-gratification and their rejection of God as Creator.

Many today will not accept that they are sinners. They do not want to accept that they must bow their knees before the God of creation. They do not want to accept that anyone has authority over them with the right to tell them what to do.

Even many in our churches do not understand what is meant when man is described as sinful. Many preachers (even many who consider themselves evangelical) think that the definition of sin can be limited to such things as adultery, alcoholism, heroin addiction, nudity, X-rated movies, and bad language. However, sin does not stop here. We must understand that sin affects every area of our lives. Sin has an influence on every aspect of our culture. We must understand that sin pervades the whole of our thinking and will, therefore, affect the whole of our actions. Jesus said, "For out of the heart proceed evil thoughts, murders, adulteries, fornications, thefts, false witness, blasphemies" (Matt. 15:19).

We must understand that God is the Creator and lawgiver, and every human must kneel in submission to Him. That there will come a time when all will do this is clearly recorded by Paul in Philippians 2:10–11: "that at the name of Jesus every knee should bow, of those in heaven, and of those on earth, and of those under the earth, and that every tongue should confess that Jesus Christ is Lord, to the glory of God the Father."

God's Word (the infallible Word of the perfect Creator) has to be the basis of our thinking. God, the Creator, is the One who provides the blueprint for happy and stable human relationships. If His Word is heeded, He supplies the basis for a true Christian philosophy for every area of human existence: agriculture, economics, medicine, politics, law enforcement, arts, music, sciences, family relationships — *every aspect of life*. In other words, there is a whole Christian way of thinking. There are foundational biblical principles that govern every area of life. The Creator has not left His creatures without an instruction manual.

"The entirety of Your word is truth" (Psalm 119:160)

Man's rejection of God as Creator (not starting with His Word as a basis for thinking in every area and not being submissive to Him) has resulted in the problems we have in society. This was painfully highlighted in the recent series of advertisements from major retail chains featuring same-sex couples. A number of major chain stores in America and around the world have begun to feature same-sex couples in an effort to show their acceptance of the homosexual lifestyle and to appeal to those living that lifestyle. One ad representative said of the stores' same-sex advertisements, "They're trying to create a modern representation of families. This reflects [the values of] a bigger, more mainstream audience than one might believe."[6] These businesses have made man the authority when it comes to moral values, specifically on what constitutes a family; therefore, their idea of a modern family is completely outside of what Scripture teaches. Of course, this is all just a reflection of how the culture in general views God's Word.

Another example of this rejection of God's Word comes from a letter to the editor of an Australian newspaper. Apparently, a country newspaper was approached for placement of an advertisement requesting a married couple for farm work. They were told there would be no printing of an advertisement that contained the words, "Married couple." The problem was apparently one of discrimination. The term "married couple" had to be replaced with "two persons." It did not matter which two persons applied for the job! The question: "On whose authority can't this be printed?" The answer: "The Human Rights Commission." The writer of the letter was justifiably horrified. However, this incident is the fruit of evolutionary thinking, and we can only expect similar instances to increase.

"Open my eyes, that I may see" (Ps. 119:18)

Concerned and convinced Christians must pray that the Lord will make clear to everyone the frightening direction in which man's rebellion is heading. Christians need to establish firmly the fact that God is Creator and that He has given us His law. We need to recognize what sin is and what the results of sinful existence are. We need to proclaim deliverance from sin through faith in Jesus Christ. Apart from this, there will be no rectifying the situation. *An all-out attack on evolutionary thinking is possibly the only real hope our nations have of rescuing themselves from an inevitable social and moral catastrophe.*

It is not easy for any human being to acknowledge that if there is a Creator we must be in submission to Him. However, there is no alternative. Man must recognize that he is in rebellion against the One who created him. Only then will man understand the law, understand

---

6. Ron Dicker, "J.C. Penney and Gap's Gay-Themed Ads Seek Profit with Progress," *Huffington Post*, http://www.huffingtonpost.com/2012/05/13/jcpenney-gap-gay-advertising_n_1510567.html#s384118&title=Stocker_Jeans.

what sin is, and understand the steps necessary to bring about the change in individual lives that can ultimately effect changes in society.

The more our society rejects the creation basis and God's laws, the more it will degenerate spiritually and morally. This has happened many times throughout history and should stand as a warning.

I also want to challenge those Christians who have re-interpreted Genesis to fit in evolutionary ideas and/or millions of years (e.g., theistic evolution; the gap theory; the day-age theory; the framework hypothesis; progressive creation; and so on). If people adopt the beliefs of secular scientists (e.g., millions of years and evolutionary beliefs) and reinterpret the clear words of Scripture, they should not be surprised if those they influence then adopt man's morality (e.g., gay marriage) and reinterpret the clear teaching in the Bible. Sadly, generations of children have grown up in a largely compromising Church that has taught them to start outside of Scripture and to re-interpret Genesis; when they start outside of Scripture and reinterpret morality, they are just being consistent

I also want to clarify an important point. There is no doubt that the increasing acceptance of evolution and/or millions of years has gone hand in hand with an increasing acceptance of gay marriage and other issues, all contributing to a rejection of biblical morality. But evolution and/or millions of years are not the cause of such happening. Obviously, sin is the ultimate cause of people rejecting God's Word. However, the teaching of evolution and/or millions of years has contributed to increasing doubt about the truthfulness of God's Word, particularly in Genesis, leading to a slippery slide of unbelief through the whole of Scripture. The more people reject God's Word as the absolute authority, the more they will become consistent and begin rejecting the morality based on the Bible, leading to increasing moral relativism — which is exactly what we see happening.

The Consequences of Rejecting God and His Absolutes

Missionaries were sent to New Guinea because there were many so-called pagan and primitive people there. The story is told of one cannibal tribe, which has since ceased to be cannibalistic. Previously, men would race into a village, grab a man by the hair, pull him back, tense his abdominal muscles, use a bamboo knife to slit open his abdomen, pull out his intestines, cut up his fingers, and while he was still alive, eat him until he died. People hear that and say, "Oh, what primitive savages!" They are not primitive savages; their ancestor was a man called Noah. The Indians' ancestor was a man called Noah; the Eskimos' ancestor was a man called Noah; and our ancestor was a man called Noah. Noah had the knowledge of God and could build ships. His ancestors could make musical instruments, and they practiced agriculture. What happened to those New Guinea natives is that, somewhere in history (as Romans 1 tells us), they rejected the knowledge of God and His laws, and God turned them over to foolish, perverse, and degenerate things.[7]

However, this same degeneracy (this same rejection of God's laws) can be seen in so-called civilized nations that cut people up alive all year long (approximately 1.2 million of them in the United States each year), and it is legalized.[8] This is what abortion is — cutting up people alive and sucking out the bits and pieces. The so-called primitive tribes had ancestors who once knew the true God and His laws. As they rejected the true God of creation, their culture degenerated in every area. The more our so-called civilized nations reject the God of creation, the more they will degenerate to a primitive culture. Thus, a culture should not be interpreted according to whether it is primitive or advanced (as presupposed by the evolutionary scale), but every aspect of a culture must be judged against the standards of God's Word. How does your nation measure up?

---

7. Although most anthropologists would deny there were or are cannibals in New Guinea, this story and others were related by missionaries who had spent most of their lives in that country. There are a number of books published documenting stories of cannibalism in New Guinea, like *Headhunter* (Sydney, Australia: Anzea Publishers, 1982).

8. According to the National Right to Life, who pulled their statistics from the Center for Disease Control (CDC) and the Guttmacher Institute, there have been 54,559,615 abortions *in the United States alone* since *Roe v. Wade* in 1973. For more detailed statistics and explanations, visit http://www.nrlc.org/Factsheets/FS03_AbortionInTheUS.pdf.

CHAPTER 7

DEATH: THE "LAST ENEMY"

Why Sin and Death?

SUPPOSE SOMEONE CAME up to you and said, "You Christians are saying that we need Jesus Christ, and that we need to confess our sins. Sin? Why do we need Christ anyway? Besides, God can't be who He says He is. If He is, like you say, a God of love, look at all the death and suffering in the world. How can that be?" What would you say?

The Gospel, Sin, and Death

What is the gospel message? When God made man, He made him perfect. He made the first two people, Adam and Eve, and placed them in the Garden of Eden, where they had a special, very beautiful relationship with God. When He made them, He gave them a choice. He wanted their love — not as a programmed response (or to be controlled like a puppet) but as a reasoned act. They chose to rebel against God. This rebellion is called sin. The origin of sin is given in the historical account of the Fall. All sin comes under the banner of rebellion against God and His will.

As a result of that rebellion in Eden, a number of things happened. First, man was estranged from God. That separation is called spiritual death. On its own, the final effect of this would have been living forever in our sinful bodies, eternally separated from God. Imagine living with Hitler and Stalin forever! Imagine living in an incorrigible, sinful state for eternity. But something else happened. Romans 5:12 tells us that as a result of man's actions came sin, and as a result of sin came death; but not just spiritual death, as some theologians claim. To confirm this, one needs only read 1 Corinthians 15:20 where Paul talks about the physical death of the *first Adam* and the physical death of Christ, the *last Adam*. Or read Genesis 3, where God expelled Adam and Eve from the Garden so that they would not eat of the Tree of Life and live forever.

What is the nature of this death? In an attempt to downplay the historical account of Adam, many Christian leaders want to explain away the Bible's first references to death. But the Bible is clear. The death that entered the human race was not only spiritual death (separation from God), but also physical death.

In Genesis 2:7 we read where life came from: "The Lord God formed man of the dust of the ground, and breathed into his nostrils the breath of life; and man became a living being." Then God's judgment on sin took away that life: "In the sweat of your face you shall eat bread till you return to the ground, for out of it you were taken; for dust you are, and to dust you shall return" (Gen. 3:19).

This definition of death as a "return to dust" is confirmed in the New Testament when Paul writes, "The first man was of the earth, made of dust . . . we have borne the image of the man of dust" (1 Cor. 15:47, 49). The book of Job also refers to death in this way: "And man would return to dust" (Job 34:15).

A church leader once said to me something like, "I believe dust-to-Adam represents molecules-to-man evolution." I then replied, "Well, what does the Bible mean when it says Adam's rib was 'made into' Eve [Gen. 2:21–22]?"

Another time, a minister said to me, "I believe the dust referred to in Genesis 2:7 represents the animal [ape-like creature] God used to form man." My response was, "Well, the Bible states we return to dust when we die, so what animal do we return to when we die?" No, when a human dies, that person's body returns to dust.

Why did God send death? Three aspects of death should be considered carefully.

1. God, as a righteous judge, cannot look upon sin. Because of His very nature and the warning He gave to Adam, God had to judge sin. He had warned Adam that if he ate of the tree of the knowledge of good and evil, "In the day that you eat of it you shall surely die" (Gen. 2:17). The Curse of death placed upon the world was, and is, a just and righteous judgment from God, who is the judge. Death is an intrusion into a once "very good" creation. In fact, the Bible calls death the "last enemy":

> The last enemy that will be destroyed is death (1 Cor. 15:26).

In the Book of Revelation, we are told that death will be thrown into the Lake of Fire — when the Curse of death is finally removed:

> Then Death and Hades were cast into the lake of fire. This is the second death (Rev. 20:14).

2. One of the aspects of man's rebellion was separation from God. The loss of a loved one through death shows the sadness of the separation between those left behind and the one who has departed this world. When we consider how sad it is when a loved one dies, it should remind us of the terrible consequences of sin that separated

Adam from the perfect relationship he had with God. This separation involved all mankind because Adam sinned as the representative of all. And because we are descendants of Adam, we inherit this sin nature; what he did, we did.

3. Another aspect of death many people miss is that God sent death as a result of sin because He loved us so much. God is love, and strange as it may sound, we should really praise Him for that Curse He placed on us. It was not God's will that man would be cut off from Him for eternity. Imagine living in a sinful state for eternity, separated from God. He loved us too much for that, and He did a very wonderful thing. In placing on us the Curse of physical death, He provided a way to redeem man back to himself. In the person of Jesus Christ, He suffered that Curse of death on the Cross for us. He tasted death for every man (Heb. 2:9). By becoming the perfect sacrifice for our sin of rebellion, He conquered death. He took the penalty that should rightly have been ours at the hands of a righteous judge and bore it in His own body on the Cross.

All who believe in Jesus Christ as Lord and Savior are received back to God to spend eternity with Him. Isn't that a wonderful message? *That is the message of Christianity.* Man forfeited his special position through sin, and as a result, God placed upon him the Curse of death so he could be redeemed back to God. What a wonderful thing God did in this righteous judgment! We need to also understand that because we committed high treason against the God of creation (when we sinned in Adam), we do not deserve to exist — we deserve nothing! But God in His mercy withdrew some of His sustaining power so that all of creation would run down (Rom. 8:22) and so our bodies would run down and die, while our souls would exist forever — eternally separated from God. But God had a plan from eternity to save us from sin and its consequence of eternal separation from Him. Every time we celebrate the Lord's Supper, we remember Christ's death and the awfulness of sin. Each time we partake of the bread and the cup, we rejoice in Christ's Resurrection and thus in the conquering of sin and death.

But evolutionary ideas and millions of years destroy the very basis of this message of love. The evolutionary process is supposed to be one of death and struggle, cruelty, brutality, and ruthlessness. It is a ghastly fight for survival, with elimination of the weak and deformed.

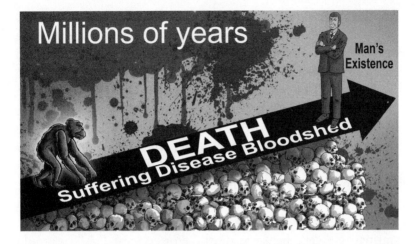

The belief in millions of years is one in which a record of death, disease, suffering, carnivory, and thorns (as observed in the fossil record) happened before man ever existed. This is what underlies evolution — death, bloodshed, and struggle bringing man into existence. Death over millions of years. It is an onward, upward "progression" leading to man. Yet what does the Bible say in Romans 5:12? Man's actions led to sin, which led to death. The Bible tells us that without the shedding of blood, there can be no remission of sin (Heb. 9:22). God instituted death and bloodshed so man could be redeemed. If death and bloodshed existed before Adam sinned, the basis for atonement is destroyed.

Evolutionists would say death and struggle led to man's existence. The Bible says man's rebellious actions led to death. These statements cannot both be true. One denies the other; they are diametrically opposed. That is why those who claim to hold both positions at the same time (theistic evolutionists) are destroying the basis of the gospel. If life formed in an onward progression, how did man fall upward? What is sin? Sin would then be an inherited animal characteristic, not something due to the fall of man through disobedience. The many Christians who accept the belief of evolution and add God to it destroy the very foundation of the gospel message they profess to believe.

At one church, a man came up to me and insisted that a Christian could believe in evolution. Since I had spent considerable time during the service showing that the Bible teaches there was no death before the Fall, I asked him whether he believed there was death before

Adam fell. In an angry tone he asked me, "Do you beat your wife?" This took me aback a little, and I was not really sure of the point he was trying to make, so I asked him what he meant by that. He asked me again, "Do you beat your wife?" Then he walked off.

Life is full of interesting experiences on the preaching trail. However, I thought about this man's comments for quite some time and then realized, after talking to a psychologist, that there is a type of question you can ask and no matter whether you answer no or yes, you are trapped. Actually, what this man should have asked me was, "Have you stopped beating your wife?" If you answer either yes or no, you are admitting that you beat your wife. In relation to the death issue and Adam's Fall, if the man had answered in the affirmative, "Yes, there was death before Adam's Fall," he would be admitting to a belief in something that contradicted the Bible. If he answered no, then he was denying evolution. Either way, he was showing that one cannot add evolution to the Bible. He was trapped, and he knew it.

I need to state here emphatically that I am not saying that if you believe in evolutionary ideas you are not a Christian. There are many Christians who, for varying reasons (whether it be out of ignorance of what evolution teaches, pride, or a liberal view of the Scriptures) believe in what evolution teaches. Those who do believe in evolutionary ideas are being inconsistent and in reality, are destroying the foundations of the gospel message. Therefore, I would plead with them to seriously consider the evidence against the position they hold.

Even atheists realize the inconsistency in Christians embracing evolutionary beliefs, as seen in a quotation from an article by G. Richard Bozarth entitled "The Meaning of Evolution":

> Christianity is — must be! — totally committed to the special creation as described in Genesis, and Christianity must fight with its full might, fair or foul, against the theory of evolution. . . . It becomes clear now that the whole justification of Jesus' life and death is predicated on the existence of Adam and the forbidden fruit he and Eve ate. Without the original sin, who needs to be redeemed? Without Adam's fall

into a life of constant sin terminated by death, what purpose is there to Christianity? None.[1]

The atheist Jacques Monod (noted for his contributions to molecular biology and philosophy) said in an interview titled "The Secret of Life," broadcast on June 10, 1976, as a tribute to him:

> Selection is the blindest, and most cruel way of evolving new species, and more and more complex and refined organisms. . . . The struggle for life and the elimination of the weakest is a horrible process, against which our whole modern ethic revolts. An ideal society is a non-selective society, it is one where the weak are protected; which is exactly the reverse of the so-called natural law. *I am surprised that a Christian would defend the idea that this is the process which God more or less set up in order to have evolution* (emphasis mine).[2]

Much more recently, the American Atheists group ran an anti-Christmas campaign. On a website promoting the campaign, the group also recognized the inconsistency of Christians who embrace evolutionary ideas:

> Chances are, if you're reading this, you don't believe in the fable of Adam and Eve and the talking snake. . . . You probably don't believe that Adam literally ate a fruit, resulting in God expelling him and Eve out of the idyllic Garden of Eden.
>
> In other words, you know that's a myth.
>
> Right so far? So if Adam and Eve and the Talking Snake are myths, then Original Sin is also a myth, right? Well, think about it. . .
>
> • Jesus' major purpose was to save mankind from Original Sin.

1. G. Richard Bozarth, "The Meaning of Evolution," *American Atheist* (February 1978): p. 30.
2. Jacques Monod, interview with Laurie John, Australian Broadcasting Co., June 10, 1976, as quoted in Henry M. Morris, *That Their Words May Be Used Against Them* (Green Forest, AR: Master Books, 1997), p. 417.

• Without Original Sin, the marketing that all people are sinners and therefore need to accept Jesus falls moot.

No Adam and Eve means no need for a savior. It also means that the Bible cannot be trusted as a source of unambiguous, literal truth. It is completely unreliable, because it all begins with a myth, and builds on that as a basis. No Fall of Man means no need for atonement and no need for a redeemer. You know it.[3]

The above statements actually show that many atheists recognize the necessity of a literal Adam and Eve and a literal Fall to the gospel better than some Christians!

Original sin, with death as a result, is the basis of the gospel. That is why Jesus Christ came and what the gospel is all about. If the First Adam is only an allegorical figure, then why not the Last Adam (1 Cor. 15:45–47), Jesus Christ? If man did not really fall into sin, there is no need for a Savior. Evolutionary ideas destroy the very foundations of Christianity because they state, "Death is, and always has been, part of life." Now, if you lived in a skyscraper, and if there were people underneath that skyscraper with jackhammers hammering away at the foundations, would you say, "So what?" Of course not, and yet that is exactly what many Christians are doing. They are being bombarded with evolution through the media, the public school system, television, and newspapers, and yet they rarely react. The foundations of the skyscraper of Christianity are being eroded by the jackhammers of evolution and millions of years. But inside the skyscraper, what are many Christians doing? They are either sitting there doing nothing or are throwing out jackhammers, saying, "Here, have a few more! Go destroy our foundations!"

Worse still, theistic evolutionists (those who believe God used evolution to create the universe and everything in it) are actively helping to undermine the basis of the gospel. As the Psalmist asks, "If the foundations are destroyed, What can the righteous do?" (Ps. 11:3). If the basis of the gospel is destroyed, the structure built on that

---

3. "Christmas," American Atheists, http://atheists.org/content/christmas.

foundation (the Christian Church) will largely collapse. If Christians wish to preserve the structure of Christianity, they must protect its foundation and therefore actively oppose evolutionary ideas.

There are many Christians who will say they do not believe in evolution because they understand that if they did, their beliefs would be in conflict with the Bible's account of Adam and Eve. However, many Christians will say that they *do* believe in millions of years. They claim that while it is important not to believe in evolution per se, it does not matter what one believes about the age of the earth.

Can a person believe in an old earth and an old universe (millions or billions of years in age) and be a Christian?

First of all, let's consider three verses that sum up the gospel and salvation. First Corinthians 15:17 says, "If Christ is not risen, your faith is futile; you are still in your sins!" Jesus said in John 3:3, "Most assuredly, I say to you, unless one is born again, he cannot see the kingdom of God." Romans 10:9 clearly explains, "If you confess with your mouth the Lord Jesus and believe in your heart that God has raised Him from the dead, you will be saved."

Numerous other passages could be cited, but not one of them states in any way that a person has to believe in a young earth or universe to be saved. And the list of those who cannot enter God's kingdom, as recorded in passages like Revelation 21:8, certainly does not include "old-earthers."

Many great men of God who are now with the Lord believed in an old earth. Some of these men explained away the Bible's clear teaching about a young earth by adopting the classic gap theory. Others accepted a day-age theory or positions such as theistic evolution, the framework hypothesis, and progressive creation.

Scripture plainly teaches that salvation is conditioned upon faith in Christ, with no requirement for what one believes about the age of the earth or universe.

Now, when I say this, people sometimes assume then that it does not matter what a Christian believes concerning the supposed age of millions of years for the earth and universe. Even though it is not a salvation issue, the belief that earth history spans millions of years has very severe implications. Let me summarize some of these.

Authority Issue

The belief in millions of years does not come from Scripture but from the fallible methods that secularists use to date the universe.

To attempt to fit millions of years into the Bible, a gap of time has to be invented that almost all Bible scholars agree the text does not allow — at least from a hermeneutical perspective. Or one has to reinterpret the days of creation as long periods of time (even though they are obviously ordinary days in the context of Genesis 1). In other words, you have to add a concept (millions of years) from outside Scripture into God's Word. This approach puts man's fallible ideas in authority over God's Word.

As soon as we surrender the Bible's authority in one area, we unlock a door to do the same thing in other areas. Once the door of compromise is open, even if ajar just a little, subsequent generations push the door open wider. Ultimately, this compromise has been a major contributing factor in the loss of biblical authority in our Western world.

The Church should heed the warning of Proverbs 30:6, "Do not add to His words, lest He rebuke you, and you be found a liar."

Contradiction Issue

A Christian's belief in millions of years totally contradicts the clear teaching of Scripture. Here are just three examples.

Thorns. Fossil thorns are found in rock layers that secularists believe to be hundreds of millions of years old, meaning they supposedly existed millions of years before man. However, the Bible makes it clear that thorns came into existence after the Curse: "Then to Adam He said, 'Because you . . . have eaten from the tree of which I commanded you, saying, "You shall not eat of it": Cursed is the ground for your sake. . . . Both thorns and thistles it shall bring forth for you'" (Gen. 3:17–18).

Disease. The fossil remains of animals, said by evolutionists to be millions of years old, show evidence of diseases (such as cancer, brain tumors, and arthritis). If these fossil remains are truly millions of years old, then we must conclude that such diseases supposedly existed millions of years before sin. Yet Scripture teaches that after

God finished creating everything and placed man at the pinnacle of creation, He described the creation as "very good" (Gen. 1:31). Certainly calling cancer and brain tumors "very good" does not fit with Scripture and the character of God.

Diet. The Bible clearly teaches in Genesis 1:29–30 that Adam and Eve and the animals were all vegetarian before sin entered the world. But we find fossil evidence showing that animals were eating each other. Evolutionists claim that these fossils are supposedly millions of years old, meaning animals were supposedly eating each other before man and thus before sin. Scripture, however, indicates clearly that animal death and carnivory did not enter the world until after the Fall.

Human and Animal Death Issue

Romans 8:22 makes it clear that the whole creation is groaning as a result of the Fall — the entrance of sin. One reason for this groaning is death — the death of living creatures, both animals and man. Death is described as an enemy (1 Cor. 15:26) that will trouble creation until the day it is thrown into the lake of fire.

Romans 5:12 and other passages make it obvious that the physical death of man (and really, death in general) entered the once-perfect creation because of man's sin. However, if a person believes that the fossil record arose over millions of years, then death, disease, suffering, carnivorous activity, and thorns existed millions of years before sin.

The first death was in the Garden of Eden when God killed an animal as the first blood sacrifice (Gen. 3:21) — a picture of what was to come in Jesus Christ, the Lamb of God, who would take away the sin of the world. Jesus Christ stepped into history to pay the penalty of sin — to conquer our enemy, death.

By dying on a Cross and being raised from the dead, Jesus conquered death and paid the penalty for sin. Although millions of years of death before sin is not a salvation issue per se, I personally believe that it is really an attack on Jesus' work on the Cross.

Recognizing that Christ's work on the Cross defeated our enemy, death, is crucial to understanding the good news of the gospel: "And God will wipe away every tear from their eyes; there shall be no more death, nor sorrow, nor crying. There shall be no more pain, for the former things have passed away" (Rev. 21:4).

Some Christians claim that the death referred to in Romans 5:12 only applies to man and not to animals. They say that as long as one believes death of humans came into existence because of sin, then a person can believe in millions of years of death of animals before man. Let's consider this in some detail.

God told Adam to eat of "every herb that yields seed" and fruit trees (Gen. 1:29). He was originally vegetarian.

Some object that God did not say Adam could not eat animal flesh, but this objection is easily dealt with by God's words to Noah after the Flood: "Every moving thing that lives shall be food for you. I have given you all things, *even as the green herbs*" (Gen. 9:3, emphasis mine). We could paraphrase: "Just as I gave you the plants to eat, now I give you all things (everything)."

This substantiates that Adam's diet was vegetarian. Not until after the Flood did God allow humans to eat animals. Adam did not eat meat, and neither did any of the animals on the earth until after sin.

But how do you respond to Christians who do not believe that Adam's diet applied to the animal world?

Genesis 1:30, written in the same way as Genesis 1:29, refers specifically to the animals: "Also, to every beast of the earth, to every bird of the air, and to everything that creeps on the earth, in which there is life, I have given every green herb for food" (Gen. 1:30).

Just as humans were vegetarian originally, the animals were also vegetarian. Before the Fall, animals did not eat animals, animals did not eat humans, and humans did not eat animals.

Yet the fossil record, which secularists claim represents millions of years of earth's history before the first man, includes examples of carnivory: bones from animals in the stomachs of other animals, fish swallowing fish, and teeth marks on bones. The fossil record also includes diseases, such as tumors and arthritis, and thorns.

If animals were vegetarian before Adam's sin, how could animals have been killing animals for millions of years before Adam? If God declared His creation "very good" before Adam's sin, how could it have included cancer and other diseases? If thorns came after the Curse (*after* Adam's sin, in Genesis 3:18), how could thorns have existed already?

Romans 8:22, written in the context of the Fall's effects, tells us, "We know that the whole creation groans and labors with birth pangs together until now." There is no way a Christian can logically and consistently allow for millions of years of animal death, violence, and disease before Adam's sin.

No, most of the fossil record is the graveyard of the Flood of Noah's day. God created a perfect world, but the world we live in today — with all its disease, death, and violence — resulted from sin. It did not exist this way for millions of years.

Taking Genesis as literal history makes it obvious that animals and humans did not die until after Adam's sin. Death is not "very good." Death is an enemy.

A Note about Plant Death

There are also those Christians who will bring up another objection, namely that when plants were eaten, the plants died; therefore, there was death before sin.

However, Scripture itself makes an important distinction between plants and animals at this point. In Genesis 1, we see a general Hebrew term — *nephesh*. This word refers to living creatures such as man and animals. The word does not apply to plants, but it does apply to vertebrates. The Bible clearly distinguishes between animals that have *nephesh* and the plants and insects, which do not. So the Bible would not classify plants as living creatures in the same way as those that have blood and flesh.

The death of creatures with *nephesh* carries a different weight, even to us as humans. If you are out in the mountains and see the form of a large sun-bleached tree stump, twisted and weathered, you might look at this dead tree and think, *Wow, that is beautiful.* We even decorate our homes with dead and dried plants. But what would the neighbors think if you decorated with the dead carcass of a dog or something? Or if you were in the woods and saw the decayed remains of an elk, would you think, *Wow, nice. Let's stop here for the picnic!* No, there is something different about animal death, isn't there?

Originally, there was no death for those who had *nephesh*. Remember, in Genesis 1:29–30 we read, "I have given you every plant . . . and it shall be food for you; and to every beast of the earth and to every bird of the sky and to everything that moves on the earth which has life, I have given every green plant for food."

Even though only plants were eaten as part of God's original creation, it was not until Genesis 9:3 — after the Flood — that God said, "Every moving thing that is alive shall be food for you; I give all to you. . . ." Somewhere between these two mandates a change occurred, but that is not the way it started. Originally, it was a beautiful world. It was exceedingly good. Pain, suffering, and death in *nephesh* animals or humans did not exist.

Not Just about a Young Earth

When I speak on these issues, people often say to me, "So you're saying we need to be young-earth creationists?"

Time and time again I have found that in both Christian and secular worlds, those of us who are involved in the creation movement are characterized as "young-earthers." The supposed battle-line is thus drawn between the "old-earthers" (this group consists of anti-God evolutionists as well as many "conservative" Christians) who appeal to what they call science versus the "young-earthers," who are said to be ignoring the overwhelming supposed scientific evidence for an old earth.

I want to make it very clear that we do not want to be known *primarily* as young-earth creationists. The biblical creation movement (involving organizations such as Answers in Genesis) and its main thrust is *not* young earth as such; the emphasis is on biblical authority. Believing in a relatively young earth (i.e., only a few thousand years old) is a consequence of accepting the authority of the Word of God over fallible man's word.

Let's be honest. Take out your Bible, and look through it. You will not be able to find any hint at all of millions or billions of years.

The biblical creation movement has published numerous quotes from many well-known and respected Christian leaders admitting that if you take Genesis in a straightforward way, it clearly teaches six ordinary days of creation. However, the reason some do not believe God created in six literal days is because they are convinced from so-called science that the world is billions of years old. In other words, they are admitting that they start *outside* the Bible to reinterpret the words of Scripture.

When someone says to me, "Oh, so you're one of those fundamentalist, young-earth creationists," I reply, "Actually, I'm a revelationist, no-death-before-Adam redemptionist!" (which really means I am a young-earth creationist).

Here is what I mean by this: I understand that the Bible is a revelation from our infinite Creator, and it is self-authenticating and self-attesting. I must interpret Scripture with Scripture, not impose ideas from the outside. When I take the plain words of the Bible, it is obvious there was no death, bloodshed, disease, or suffering of humans or animals before sin. God instituted death and bloodshed because of sin; this is foundational to the gospel. Therefore, one cannot allow a fossil record of millions of years of death, bloodshed, disease, and suffering before sin (which is why the fossil record makes much more sense as the graveyard of the Flood of Noah's day).

Also, the word for *day* in the context of Genesis can only mean an ordinary day for each of the six days of creation.[4]

Thus, as a revelationist, I let God's Word speak to me, with the words' meaning being derived according to the context of the language they were written in. Once I accept the plain words of Scripture in context, the fact of ordinary days, no death before sin, the Bible's genealogies, and so on all make it clear that I cannot accept millions or billions of years of history. Therefore, I would conclude there must be something wrong with fallible man's ideas about the age of the universe.

And the fact is, every single dating method (outside of Scripture) is based on fallible assumptions. There are literally hundreds of dating tools. However, whatever dating method one uses, assumptions must be made about the past. Not one dating method man devises is absolute. Even though 90 percent of all dating methods give dates far younger than evolutionists require, none of these can be used in an absolute sense either.[5]

Question: Why would any Christian want to take man's fallible dating methods and use them to impose an idea on the *infallible* Word

---

4. For more on the word day in Genesis, see Terry Mortenson, "Six Literal Days," Answers in Genesis, http://www.answersingenesis.org/articles/am/v5/n2/six-literal-days.
5. For more on the flaws in dating methods, see Roger Patterson, *Evolution Exposed* (Hebron, KY: Answers in Genesis, 2006), p. 105–130; available online at http://www.answersingenesis.org/articles/ee2/dating-methods.

of God? Christians who accept billions of years are in essence saying that man's word is infallible but God's Word is fallible!

This is the crux of the issue. When Christians have agreed with the world that they can accept man's fallible dating methods to interpret God's Word, they have agreed with the world that the Bible cannot be trusted. They have essentially sent out the message that man, by himself, independent of revelation, can determine truth and impose this on God's Word. Once this door has been opened regarding Genesis, ultimately it can happen with the rest of the Bible. It is an issue of authority. Who is the ultimate authority — God or man?

You see, if Christian leaders have told the next generation that they can accept the world's teachings concerning origins in geology, biology, astronomy, and so on and use these to reinterpret God's Word, then the door has been opened for this to happen in *every* area, including morality.

Yes, one can be a conservative Christian and preach authoritatively from God's Word from Genesis 12 onward. But once you have told people to accept man's dating methods and thus not to take the first chapters of Genesis as they are written, you have effectively undermined the Bible's authority! This attitude is destructive to the Church.

So the issue is not young earth versus old earth, but this: Can fallible, sinful man be in authority over the Word of God?

A young-earth view admittedly receives the scoffing from a majority of the scientists. But Paul warned us in 1 Corinthians 8:2, "And if anyone thinks that he knows anything, he knows nothing yet as he ought to know." Compared to what God knows, we know next door to nothing! This is why we should be so careful to let God speak *to* us through His Word and not try to impose our ideas *on* God's Word.

It is also interesting to note that this verse is found in the same passage where Paul warns that "knowledge puffs up." Academic pride is found throughout our culture. Therefore, many Christian leaders would rather believe the world's fallible academics than the simple, clear words of the Bible.

I believe this message needs to be proclaimed to the Church as a challenge to return to biblical authority and thus stand tall in the world for the inerrancy of God's Word. Ultimately, this is the only way we are going to reach the world with the truth of the gospel message.

We need to put more pressure on our Christian leaders to take a long, hard look at how they are approaching the question of the authority of the Bible!

Rooted in Genesis

To summarize and recap what we have been discussing thus far in this book, all biblical doctrines, including the gospel itself, are ultimately rooted in the first book of the Bible.

- God specially created everything in heaven and earth (Gen. 1:1).

- God uniquely created men and women in His image (Gen. 1:26–27).

- Marriage consists of one man and one woman for life (Gen. 2:24).

- The first man and woman brought sin into the world (Gen. 3:1–24).

- From the beginning God promised a Messiah to save us (Gen. 3:15).

- Death and suffering arose because of original sin (Gen. 3:16–19).

- God sets society's standards of right and wrong (Gen. 6:5–6).

- The ultimate purpose of life is to walk with God (Gen. 6:9–10).

- All people belong to one race — the human race (Gen. 11:1–9).

New Heavens and New Earth
Paradise Restored

Evolution and/or millions of years also destroy the teaching of the new heavens and the new earth. What are we told about the new heavens and the new earth? Acts 3:21 says there will be a restoration (restitution) — things will be restored to at least what they were originally.

In Genesis, we find that man and animals were told to eat only plants (Gen. 1:29–30); they were vegetarians. Only after the Flood was man told he could eat meat (Gen. 9:3). There were only vegetarians when God first created, and there was no violence, death, or disease before Adam sinned.

To believe in evolution and/or millions of years is to deny a universal paradise before Adam, because evolution necessarily implies that before Adam there was struggle, cruelty and brutality, animals eating animals, and death. Is the world going to be restored to that? Thus if you believe in evolution and/or millions of years, you must deny a universal paradise before Adam (because you believe that there was death and struggle millions of years before Adam), and also at the end of time (because the Bible teaches the world will be restored to what it used to be). Thus, evolution and millions of years not only strike at the heart and the foundation but at the hope of Christianity as well.

Also, Christians who do believe in evolution and millions of years must accept that evolution is still going on. In fact, evolutionists actually teach this.[6] This is because evolutionists use the death and struggle

---

6. An online *Time* magazine article, in response to a study on natural selection, declares, "Modern *Homo sapiens* Is Still Evolving." See Eben Harrell, "Darwin Lives! Modern Humans Are Still Evolving," *Time Science*, http://www.time.com/time/health/article/0,8599,1931757,00.html.

we see in the world and mutations (mistakes in the genes) that occur to try to prove that evolution is possible. They extrapolate into the past what they see today and deduce that these processes over millions of years are the basis for evolution. Christians who accept evolutionary ideas must agree, therefore, that evolution is occurring today in every area, including in man. However, God has said in His Word that when He created everything He finished His work of creation and pronounced it "very good" (Gen. 1:31–2:3). This is completely contrary to what evolutionists are telling us. Theistic evolutionists cannot say that God once used evolution and now does not. To say that evolution is not occurring today is to destroy evolutionary belief, as there is no basis for saying it ever happened in the past.

There are many Christians who, after being taught the true nature of science and that evolution and millions of years have their belief (religious) aspects, abandon beliefs such as theistic evolution and progressive creation. However, there are a number of ministers, theologians, and others who, because of their whole view of Scripture, will not accept what we are saying. They have a basic philosophical disagreement with us in regard to how to approach the Bible.

Perhaps the best way to summarize this argument is to give a practical example from an encounter I had with a Protestant church minister.

Many years ago, the creation ministry I was a founder of in Australia had personnel travel to the state of Victoria to conduct meetings in various centers. In one location, this minister opposed us publicly. Another minister, in the same church, had put an advertisement in the church's weekly announcement sheet concerning our visit. The opposing minister deleted the advertisement before the sheet was printed. He encouraged people to boycott our seminar program and made many discouraging public statements concerning our organization and teachings. He even told people that we were of the devil and they should not listen to us.

I made an appointment with this minister to discuss the issue with him. He explained that he believed Genesis was only symbolic, that there were a great many mistakes in the Bible, and that one could not take it as literally, as I appeared to do. The reason we had this disagreement concerning creation/evolution/age of the earth was because we had a basic philosophical disagreement regarding our personal approach to the Scriptures. He agreed this was so but again emphasized one could not take Genesis literally and that it was only symbolic. I asked him whether he believed that God created the heavens and the earth.

He said, "Yes, this was the message that Genesis was teaching."

Deliberately, I quoted Genesis 1:1, "Do you believe, 'In the beginning God created the heavens and earth?' "

He said, "Yes, of course I do. That is the message Genesis is getting across to us."

I explained to him that he had just taken Genesis 1:1 literally. He was asked whether Genesis 1:1 was symbolic, and, if not, why did he take it literally. I then asked whether Genesis 1:2 was literal or symbolic. I pointed out the inconsistency of accepting Genesis 1:1 as literal but saying the whole of Genesis was symbolic. He went on to say it was not important what Genesis said; only what it meant was important.

"How can you ever understand the meaning of anything if you do not know what it says?" I asked. "If you cannot take what it says to arrive at the meaning, then the English (or any other) language really becomes nonsense."

I then asked him how he decided what was truth concerning the Scriptures. He replied, "By a consensus of opinion amongst the fellowship."

So I said, "This, then, is your basis for deciding what truth is. Where did you get this basis from, and how do you know that this is the right basis for deciding truth?"

He looked at me and said, "By a consensus of opinion among scholars."

I again posed the question to him, "If this, now, is your basis for deciding truth and determining whether or not your fellowship has come to the right conclusion about truth, how do you know that this is the right basis to determine what truth is?"

He then told me that he did not have all day to talk about this topic, and it was best we now finish the discussion. What he was doing, of course, was appealing to man's wisdom to decide what Scripture meant or said, rather than allowing God's Word to tell him what the truth was. The real difference between our positions could be summed up as follows: *Where do you put your faith — in the words of men who are fallible creatures, who do not know everything, and who were not there — or the Words of God who is perfect, who knows everything, and who was there?*

Christians (or those professing to be Christian) who take this compromised view of Scripture will more often than not see the results of this wrong philosophy in the next generation: their children — and the coming generations of young people in the Church. Because they cannot provide a solid foundation for their children, parents frequently see the whole structure of Christianity collapsing in the next generation. For many of these people, it is sad but true that most of their children will reject Christianity completely. Today in the United States, we see two-thirds of young people leaving the Church by the time they reach college age — and research indicates that Christian leaders teaching millions of years and compromising Scriptures to fit this in is a significant contributing factor.[7] This dilemma is very much related to the controversy concerning Genesis. If one rejects Genesis, claims it is only symbolism or myth, or alleges that it does not mean what it clearly states, this logically leads to a slippery slide of unbelief through the rest of Scripture.

This is reflected in those who have a liberal approach to theology and try to explain away the miracles, such as the crossing of the Red Sea, the burning bush, or a fish swallowing a man (to name but a few). But these people do not stop there. They go on to explain away the miracles of Christ in the New Testament. Sometimes (and increasingly so) even the Virgin Birth and the Resurrection are denied. Once one accepts Genesis as literal and understands it as being foundational for the rest of Scripture, it is an easy step to accepting as truth the remainder of what the Bible says. Even for those who are conservative in their approach to Scripture but compromise Genesis with millions of years, this will create doubt in regard to trusting God's Word — doubt that can lead to unbelief in God's Word.

---

7. Ken Ham and Britt Beemer, *Already Gone: Why Your Kids Will Quit the Church and What You Can Do to Stop It*, with Todd Hillard (Green Forest, AR: Master Books, 2009).

I take the Bible literally (or naturally — according the type of literature/context) unless it is obviously symbolic. Even where it is symbolic, the words and phrases used have a literal basis.

Many people use the example in Scripture where it says that Jesus is the door to say that we cannot take that literally. However, understanding the customs of the times, we find that the shepherd used to sit in the gate and literally be the door. So in this sense, Jesus is literally the door, just as the shepherd literally was the door. We use such language in our everyday speech, but it is easy to recognize when one is using something symbolically. For instance, we might say, "It is raining cats and dogs." We know exactly what this means because we understand the symbolism and context — it is raining very heavily. As Christians we might pray, "Lord, please open a door for us to know which direction we should go" — and we know exactly what that means.

Too many people are quick to jump to conclusions concerning the literalness of Scripture without carefully considering the statement, the context, and the customs. When Scripture is meant to be taken symbolically or metaphorically, it is either obviously so from the context or we are told so.

Of course, many Christian academics claim that the biblical creation ministry is divisive. In that claim they certainly are correct; the truth always divides. As Christ said, He came with a sword to divide: "For I have come to 'set a man against his father, a daughter against her mother, and a daughter-in-law against her mother-in-law'" (Matt. 10:35). How many situations do you know where relationships have been broken because of the tension between living as a Christian and not living as one? Compromise is too often made with the Christian giving ground for the sake of peace and harmony. Jesus predicted strife, not peace at any price. In Luke 12:51, Jesus said, "Do you suppose that I came to give peace on earth? I tell you, not at all, but rather division" (see also John 7:12, 43; 9:16; 10:19).

From a practical perspective, I find that students do not want somebody telling them the Bible is full of mistakes that cause them to doubt or that they cannot believe it. They want to hear that there are answers and that they can really know. They respond when one preaches with authority.

At one meeting a mother told me that her daughter was in the class I had spoken to at the local public school. Her daughter had told her that the thing that impressed the students more than anything was the fact that I spoke with such authority. They were impressed that I did not question God's Word but totally accepted it. It reminded me of the statement in the Scriptures: "the people were astonished at His teaching, for He taught them as one having authority, and not as the scribes" (Matt. 7:28–29). Jesus was very authoritative and very dogmatic in the way He spoke. He did not preach various ways into heaven. He did not come and say that He believed He was one of the ways to eternal life. Jesus said, "I am *the* Way, *the* Truth and *the* Life" (John 14:6, emphasis mine). I do not think Jesus would be accepted in many churches today if He were to preach. He would be considered too divisive or even intolerant! It was little different 2,000 years ago. Are we, as born-again Christians, who are the embodiment of Christ on earth today, too scared to proclaim the truth in case we are divisive or accused of being intolerant?

I spoke to one particular church youth group on the importance of Genesis. I was amazed at the youth leader, who, at the end of the program, told the young people how disappointed he was with my low view of Scripture. He said that I was trying to impose a perfect Bible on God and explained how inadequate this view of Scripture was. They, on the other hand, were prepared to accept that there were mistakes and problems in the Bible. This led to a very high view of Scripture. After this conversation, I decided that words were meaningless for this person.

Many people (particularly those of the younger generation) have commented on the lack of authoritative teaching. It is a sad indictment upon our Church. What are they feeding their people? Our church leaders must preach with authority that God made man; that man fell in the Garden of Eden, bringing sin and death into the world; and that man finds redemption by faith in Christ alone.

CHAPTER 8

THE EVIL FRUIT OF EVOLUTIONARY THINKING

IF YOU ACCEPT A BELIEF IN GOD as Creator, then you accept that there are laws, since He is the lawgiver. God's law is the reflection of His holy character. He is the absolute authority, and we are under total obligation to Him. Laws are not a matter of our opinions but are rules given by the One who has the right to impose them upon us for our good and for His own glory. He gives us principles as a basis for building our thinking in every area.

Accepting the God of creation tells us what life is all about. We know that God is the life-giver, that life has meaning and purpose, and that all humans are created in the image of God and therefore, are of great value and significance. *God made us so He could relate to us, love us, and pour out His blessing on us and so that we could love Him in return.*

On the other hand, if you reject God and replace Him with another belief that puts chance and random processes in the place

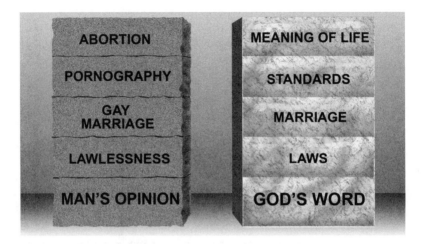

of God, there is no basis for right or wrong. Rules become whatever you want to make them. There are no absolutes — no principles that must be adhered to. People will write their own rules.

It must be understood that our worldview is built on our starting point — either God's Word or man's word.

Our Western world has by and large been permeated by a reasonably Christianized worldview, greatly influenced by the starting point of God's Word (the Bible). But as more and more people in a nation change their starting point from God's Word to man's word, we would expect to see (and are seeing) a change in the worldview of that culture. The culture is changing from one permeated by Christian absolutes (e.g., marriage is one man for one woman, abortion outlawed as murder, and so on) to one of moral relativism (e.g., marriage redefined to allow for same-sex unions, abortion legalized as a woman's right, and so on). In fact, consider just some of the changes that have occurred in the United States:

- In 1962, school prayer was ruled unconstitutional.

- In 1963, Bible reading in public schools was ruled unconstitutional.

- In 1973, restrictions on abortion were lifted, and abortion clinics began to permeate the nation (*Roe v. Wade*).

- In 1985, nativity scenes in public places were ruled to violate the so-called separation of church and state.

- In 2003, laws against homosexual sodomy were ruled unconstitutional.

Many Christians recognize the degeneration that has occurred in society. They see the collapse in Christian ethics and the increase in anti-God philosophies. They are well aware of the increase of lawlessness, homosexual behavior, pornography, and abortion (and other products of secular humanistic philosophy), but they are at a loss to know why this is occurring. The reason they are in such a dilemma is that they do not understand the foundational nature of the battle. God's Word versus man's word is the bottom line. But many Christians do not understand that the teaching of evolution and/or millions of years basically as fact in the culture, and the increasing acceptance of such beliefs by the Church (including Church leaders, Christian academics, and the general Church population as a whole), is what is contributing to this change.

What has happened is that the authority of God's Word has been undermined, and wittingly or unwittingly, because of such compromise with man's belief in evolutionary ideas and millions of years, there has been a generational loss in people's respect for and belief in the Bible. More and more of those in our coming generations (even from the Church) have been led to doubt and even reject the Bible's history and consequently have rejected the morality (and the gospel) built on that history.

Recap of the Real Issue

It is important to understand that evolutionary beliefs and millions of years are not the direct cause of social issues like gay marriage, abortion, and so on. Sin is the cause of such things. However, there is a connection between evolution/millions of years and these moral issues. The more people believe in evolution and/or millions of years, and the more they reject the infallibility of God's Word beginning in Genesis, the more they will also begin to doubt Scripture and to reject the morality built on God's Word. Also, the more young people in the Church are led to believe they can start outside the Bible with man's fallible ideas, such as evolution and millions of years, the more they will be consistent and take man's fallible ideas about morality and reinterpret what the Bible clearly teaches about such matters.

When Christians reinterpret the days of creation to fit with millions of years, reinterpret Genesis 1:1 to fit with the big bang, or adopt other positions that add Darwinian evolution to the Bible, they are undermining the very Word of God itself. And this undermining is the issue; this is why we have lost biblical authority in the culture.

As I often remind Christians, we know that Jesus rose from the dead because we take God's Word as it is written. Secular scientists have never shown that a dead body can be raised to life, but we do not reinterpret the Resurrection as a nonliteral event. We take God's Word as written.

Yet in Genesis, so many Christians (including numerous Christian leaders) accept secular scientists' old-earth ideas and reinterpret the creation account. In so doing, they have unlocked a door — the door to undermining biblical authority. Subsequent generations usually push that door open further. This is what has happened across Europe, the United Kingdom, and Australia, and it is happening across America as well.

Psalm 11:3 states, "If the foundations are destroyed, what can the righteous do?" Applied to where we are today, the foundational issues are not ultimately creation/evolution and millions of years but God's Word versus man's word. This is the same battle that began in Genesis 3:1 when the serpent said to the woman, "Has God indeed said . . . ?"

That sums up what the creation/evolution/millions of years battle is really all about; it is about authority. God's infallible Word or man's fallible word — who is the ultimate authority?

The Fruit of Evolutionary Thinking

As evolution is by and large taught as fact in the secular education systems of the world, I want to give some specific examples of how people have used evolution as their justification for their ungodly beliefs and behavior.

It is important not to misunderstand what I am saying. Certainly, evil, anti-God philosophies existed before Darwinian evolution. People aborted babies before Darwin popularized his view of evolution.

However, what people believe about where they came from does affect their worldview. When people reject the God of creation, it affects how they view themselves, others, and the world in which they live.

Particularly in Western nations, where Christian ethics were once very prevalent, Darwinian evolution provided a justification for people not to believe in God and therefore, to do those things Christians would deem wrong. As Richard Dawkins once wrote, "Although atheism might have been logically tenable before Darwin, Darwin made it possible to be an intellectually fulfilled atheist."[1] Or as one non-Christian scientist said in an interview, "Darwinian evolution helped make atheism respectable."

We are now going to consider a number of areas where evolution has been used to justify people's attitudes and actions. This does not mean that Darwinian evolution is the cause of these attitudes or actions but rather has been used by people as a justification to make their particular philosophy respectable in their eyes.

1. Nazism and Evolution

Much has been written about one of fascism's more infamous sons, Adolf Hitler. His treatment of Jews may be attributed, at least in part, to his belief in evolution. P. Hoffman, in *Hitler's Personal Security*, said, "Hitler believed in struggle as a Darwinian principle of human life that forced every people to try to dominate all others; without struggle they would rot and perish. . . . Even in his own defeat in April 1945, Hitler expressed his faith in the survival of the stronger and declared the Slavic peoples to have proven themselves the stronger."[2]

Sir Arthur Keith, the well-known evolutionist, explains how Hitler was only being consistent in what he did to the Jews; he was applying the principles of Darwinian evolution. In *Evolution and Ethics*, he said:

> To see evolutionary measures and tribal morality being applied vigorously to the affairs of a great modern nation,

---

1. Richard Dawkins, *The Blind Watchmaker: Why the Evidence of Evolution Reveals a Universe without Design* (New York: W.W. Norton, 1986), p. 6.
2. Peter Hoffman, *Hitler's Personal Security* (Oxford, England: Pergamon Press, 1979), p. 264.

we must turn again to Germany of 1942. We see Hitler devoutly convinced that evolution produces the only real basis for a national policy. . . . The means he adopted to secure the destiny of his race and people were organized slaughter, which has drenched Europe in blood. . . . Such conduct is highly immoral as measured by every scale of ethics, yet Germany justifies it; it is consonant with tribal or evolutionary morality. Germany has reverted to the tribal past, and is demonstrating to the world, in their naked ferocity, the methods of evolution.[3]

2. Racism and Evolution

The late Stephen J. Gould said:

Recapitulation [the evolutionary theory which postulates that a developing embryo in its mother's womb goes through evolutionary stages, such as the fish stage, etc., until it becomes human] provided a convenient focus for the pervasive racism of white scientists; they looked to the activities of their own children for comparison with normal, adult behavior in lower races (brackets mine).[4]

Gould also concludes that the term *mongoloid* became synonymous with mentally defective people because it was believed the Caucasian race was more highly developed than the Mongoloid. Therefore, some thought that a mentally defective child was really a throwback to a previous stage in evolution.

Gould also stated, "Biological arguments for racism may have been common before 1859, but they increased by orders of magnitude following the acceptance of evolutionary theory."[5]

The leading American paleontologist of the first half of the 20th century, Henry Fairfield Osborn, adds fuel to the fire with his belief: "The Negroid stock is even more ancient than the Caucasian and Mongolian. . . . The standard of intelligence of the average adult

3. Sir Arthur Keith, *Evolution and Ethics* (New York: Putnam, 1947), p. 28.
4. Stephen J. Gould, *The Panda's Thumb: More Reflections in Natural History* (New York: W. W. Norton, 1980), p. 163.
5. Gould, *Ontogeny and Phylogeny* (Cambridge, MA: Belknap Press, 1977), p. 127.

Negro is similar to that of the eleven-year-old youth of the species *Homo sapiens*."[6]

Many of the early settlers of Australia considered the Australian Aborigines to be less intelligent than the white man because in the settlers' view, aborigines had not evolved as far as whites on the evolutionary scale. In fact, the Hobart Museum in Tasmania (Australia) in 1984 listed this as one of the reasons why early white settlers killed as many aborigines as they could in that state. In 1924, the *New York Tribune* (Sunday, February 10) had a very large article telling their readers that the missing link had been found in Australia. The missing link referred to happened to be aborigines from the state of Tasmania.

Where would any group of people get the idea that one race is less evolved than another? Prominent scientists, such as Osborn above, promoted this idea! Ernst Haeckel, a well-known German biologist in the mid-19th century, argued for 12 races of man, each distinguished by three factors: skin color, hair type, and skull structure.[7] Regarding what he called the "lowest and most ape-like men" and the "most highly developed men," Haeckel argued in favor of his proposed lower races being equivalent to animals:

> If one must draw a sharp boundary line between them, it has to be drawn between the most highly developed and civilized man on the one hand, and the rudest savages on the other, and the latter have to be classed with the animals. This is, in fact, the opinion of many travellers, who have long watched the lowest human races in their native countries. Thus for example, a great English traveller, who lived for a considerable time on the west coast of Africa, says: "I consider the Negro to be a lower species of man, and cannot make up my mind to look upon him as 'a man and a brother,' for the gorilla would then also have to be admitted into the family."[8]

---

6. Henry F. Osborn, "The Evolution of Human Races," *Natural History* 26, no. 1 (January–February 1926): 5.
7. Ernst Haeckel, *The History of Creation*, E. Ray Lancaster, translator (London: Henry S. King & Co., 1876), 2:306.
8. Ibid., 2:365.

The incredible thing is that we live in a society that states it wants to be rid of racist attitudes. Yet we are conditioned to racist attitudes by our very education system, and the whole foundational basis for racism permeates people's minds. At one school I was at years ago, a teacher said to her students that if ape-like creatures had evolved into people, then this should be seen to be happening today. Some of the students told her that this was happening today because some aborigines are primitive and therefore, still evolving. Regrettably, in the children's eyes, the teaching of evolution had relegated the Australian Aborigines to a sub-human level.

It was the evolutionary view that convinced anthropologists there were different races of humans at different levels of intelligence and ability. It is the Christian view that teaches there is one race (in the sense that we all came from the same two humans, and therefore there are no lower or higher evolutionary groups) and that all people are equal. Sadly, today it is the secular world and not the Christian world that is leading the way in telling people there are no biological races within humankind — only different cultural groups belonging to one race.

For instance, when the Human Genome Project mapped the human genome, their results confirmed the fact that there are no biological races:

> Dr. Venter and scientists at the National Institutes of Health recently announced that they had put together a draft of the entire sequence of the human genome, and the researchers had unanimously declared, there is only one race — the human race.[9]

How has the secular word reacted to these conclusions? In 2011, William Leonard, editor of *The American Biology Teacher*, wrote in an article, ". . . all humans are one race: *Homo sapiens*. There is absolutely no genetic or evolutionary justification for 'racial' categories of humans."[10]

---

9. Natalie Angier, "Do Races Differ? Not Really, Genes Show," *The New York Times*, August 22, 2000, http://www.nytimes.com/2000/08/22/science/do-races-differ-not-really-genes-show.html?pagewanted=all&src=pm.

10. William Leonard, "Check Your Race in the Box Below," *The American Biology Teacher* 73, no. 7 (2011): 379.

Ian Tattersall, an anthropologist and curator at the American Museum of Natural History (AMNH), and Rob DeSalle, an adjunct professor of evolutionary biology and also a curator at AMNH, wrote in their recent book on race, "The principal common thread running through this chapter is the uncertainty that continues to accompany just what is signified by the word 'race,' a term that we would be much better off without but that has so far resisted expulsion from our vocabularies."[11] These statements from secular researchers directly contradict what Darwinian evolution teaches about race. Christians should be at the forefront of teaching that there are no biological races, only different people groups.[12]

3. Drugs and Evolution

Many people would not think of evolution as being in any way related to the taking of drugs. However, the following letter of testimony from a man in Western Australia shows clearly this relationship.

> At school, the theory of evolution was presented in such a way that none of us ever doubted it was scientific fact. Although the school was supposedly Christian, the biblical account of creation was presented as a kind of romantic fiction, not intended to convey literal truths about God, man, or the cosmos. As a result, I assumed the Bible was unscientific and therefore practically of little or no use.
>
> It never occurred to me that evolution was only an assumption — a concept concocted in someone's head — and I regret to say that I wasn't sufficiently interested to go check out the so-called facts for myself. I assumed that reliable people had already done that.
>
> After I left school, I began to put into practice the assumptions and presuppositions I'd picked up during childhood. My naive belief in evolution had three important practical consequences:

---

11. Ian Tattersall and Rob DeSalle, *Race? Debunking a Scientific Myth* (College Station, TX: Texas A&M University Press, 2011), p. 55.
12. For more on a biblical view of race, see Ken Ham and Charles Ware, *One Race, One Blood: A Biblical Answer to Racism* (Green Forest, AR: Master Books, 2010).

1. It strongly encouraged me to look to drugs as an ultimate source of comfort and creativity.

2. It led me to the conclusion that God, if He was around at all, was a very distant and impersonal figure, separated from humanity by very great distances of space and time.

3. It led me to increasingly abandon the moral values I had been taught at home, because when man is viewed as an arbitrary by-product of Time + Matter + Chance, there is no logical reason for treating men or women as objects of dignity and respect, since in principle they are no different from the animals, trees, and rocks from which they supposedly came.

I want to elaborate on just one point, the great faith in dope that I had as a result of being convinced that evolution was fact. After leaving school, I became increasingly susceptible to drugs. Drug-taking seemed to me to make sense because in principle it fitted with what I'd been taught about the nature and origin of man. "From chemical reactions hast thou come, and unto chemicals thou shalt return." And so I did.

My faith in drugs as a source of comfort and creativity was almost unbreakable even after ten years of total devastation, during which my job, personality, and relationships had fallen apart. Even after I came to Christ, I still continued using drugs, or feeling strongly drawn to them, until some Christians had pointed out the truth about man's nature, origin, and destiny as recounted in Genesis. It was only when I perceived the truth of this that my private love of drugs was completely and voluntarily abandoned. *I now know that my hope is in the person of Jesus Christ and in Him only. It's no longer a platitude but a living reality. I'm free, and it is the truth that has made me free — free from any desire for dope, free from the compelling faith I once had in chemicals as a result of believing a lie — the lie of evolution.* I appeal to you parents and teachers to reexamine the evidence as I have done.

4. Abortion and Evolution

Many will remember being taught in school that as an embryo develops in its mother's womb, it goes through a fish stage with gill slits and so forth, and it continues through other evolutionary stages until it becomes human. In other words, the idea is that as the embryo develops it passes through all the evolutionary stages reflecting its ancestry. This belief in embryonic recapitulation was promoted Ernst Haeckel. Not many people realize that this whole idea was an intentional deception. I quote, "But it still remains true that, in attempting to prove his law, Haeckel resorted to a series of dishonest distortions in making his illustrations. Branding them as dishonest is not too harsh, since Haeckel mentions where he originally procured some of his drawings without mentioning the alterations he made."[13]

Eventually, Ernst Haeckel admitted this fraud, but the deplorable aspect is that this theory is still taught in many universities, schools, and colleges throughout the world. Admittedly, evolutionists who have kept up with the latest writings know that this view is wrong and refrain from teaching it in their classes. However, in most of the popular school textbooks and reading materials this view is still promulgated in various forms, often very subtly — even in the 21st century.

As people accepted the idea that the child developing in a mother's womb was just an animal reflecting its evolutionary ancestry, there was less and less problem with destroying it. As evolutionary ideas became more accepted, it became easier to accept abortion. In fact, I had a lady in the United States tell me about an abortion clinic that took women aside to explain to them that what is being aborted is simply an embryo in the fish stage of evolution and that the embryo must not be thought of as human. These women are being fed outright lies.

Again, let me state here that abortion certainly existed before Darwin popularized his evolutionary ideas. However, his evolutionary belief has been used to give abortion supposed respectability in certain people's thinking. And think about it! The more generations of people that are told what is developing in a woman's womb is just an animal (because all humans are supposedly just animals — apes), the more people will think of unborn babies like spare cats: if you get rid of

---

13. Wilbert H. Rusch, Sr., "Ontogeny Recapitulates Phylogeny," *Creation Research Society 1969 Annual* 6, no. 1 (1969): 28.

spare cats, why not get rid of spare humans by abortion? After all, if humans are just animals, why does it ultimately matter what happens?

5. Business Methods and Evolution

In the last half of the 19th century, a widespread philosophy known as social Darwinism dominated the thinking of many industrial tycoons of the era. They believed that because evolution was true in the biological sphere, the same methods should apply in the business world: survival of the fittest, elimination of the weak, and no love for the poor.

In 1985 one of Australia's large banks (the National Australia Bank), in a commemorative magazine concerning their merging with another bank, used Darwinian principles of survival of the fittest to justify its merger.

More recently, a media company's overhaul from print to online-only publishing was said to be "about embracing the Darwinian concept of the survival of the fittest," because "it is virtually certain that physical daily newspapers will go the way of dinosaurs."[14] Even in American politics, politicians identify the principals of social Darwinism and survival of the fittest in each other's policies. Ironically, this identification is often meant negatively.[15] There are many other examples in history books of famous businessmen who have accepted evolutionary ideas and applied them in the business field.

6. Male Chauvinism and Evolution

Many try to blame Christianity for the chauvinist attitude of many males in our society. They claim the Bible teaches that men are superior to women and that women are not equal to men. This, of course, is not true. The Bible teaches that men and women are equal, but they have different roles because of the way God created them and because of their reactions to the temptation of the serpent (1 Tim. 2:12–14). In *New Scientist,* Evelleen Richards states, "In a period when women were beginning to demand the suffrage, higher

---

14. Adele Ferguson, "Fairfax Changes Have Some Way to Run," *Sydney Morning Herald,* http://m.smh.com.au/business/fairfax-changes-have-some-way-to-run-20120618-20jfn.html.

15. Sharon Cohen, "Fair Shot or Freedom? Words Define Campaign 2012," *Businessweek,* http://www.businessweek.com/ap/2012-06/D9VEAMS00.htm.

education and entrance to middle-class professions, it was comforting to know that women could never outstrip men; the new Darwinism scientifically guaranteed it." She went on in the article to say, ". . . an evolutionary reconstruction that centers on the aggressive, territorial, hunting male and relegates the female to submissive domesticity and the periphery of the evolutionary process."[16] In other words, some have used Darwinian evolution to justify that females are inferior. However, there are those in the feminist movement today who use evolution to try to justify that females are superior. There are even those who use evolution to justify children's rights. When you think about this, any idea that justifies either male or female supremacy justifies neither.

Christian women need to realize that the radical secular feminist and evangelical feminist movements are pervaded by evolutionist philosophy. Christian women need to be alert and not be deceived by such an anti-God movement.

How Do Christians Change the Culture?

A whole book could be written about the justification of many of the evils we see today from a foundational acceptance of evolutionary philosophy. But again people ask, "Are you blaming evolution for all the evils in society?" My answer is, "Yes and no." No — because it is not primarily evolution/millions of years that are to blame but the rejection of God's Word as the absolute authority. As people reject God's Word as their starting point and build their worldview on the starting point of man's word, they abandon Christian ethics and accept beliefs in accordance with their own opinions. Yes — because, in a very real sense, the justification for people rejecting the God of creation is the so-called scientific view of evolution. Evolution and its foundation of millions of years is the main justification today for rejecting belief in God's Word in Genesis and ultimately for many, rejecting belief in God as Creator.

The following illustration, which we refer to as the "castle diagram," is my favorite, and it beautifully summarizes what this book is all about; it illustrates the problem in our culture.

---

16. Evelleen Richards, "Will the Real Charles Darwin Please Stand Up?" New Scientist, December 22/29, 1983, p. 887.

On the left, we see the foundation of man's word. The castle built upon it represents the secular humanistic worldview. Out of this worldview come the social issues (gay marriage, abortion, and so on) we have been discussing. On the right, we see the foundation of God's Word, and built upon that is the castle representing the biblical worldview (doctrines, gospel, and so on). As part of the foundation of God's Word is attacked (by both the secularists and Christians who compromise God's Word with evolution/millions of years), the structure starts to collapse. On the Christian structure, the cannons are either aimed at each other, aimed nowhere, or aimed at the social issues.

Many might even agree to fight against such issues as abortion, gay marriage, sexual immorality, pornography, and so on. But if we attack only at the level of these issues and not the motivation for their popularity, we are not going to be successful. Even if the laws are changed in our society to outlaw abortion and gay marriage, the next generation, which is more secularized, will simply change the law again. One really cannot legislate morality — such is dependent on hearts and minds. If the Church wants to be successful in changing society's attitudes toward abortion and gay marriage, it is going to have to fight the issue at a foundational level.

It is important to understand that these moral issues are really the symptoms — not the problem. Christians in the United States have spent millions of dollars trying to change the culture (deal with these social issues), but it has not worked. Why not? Because the Bible does not say to go into all the world and change the culture. The Bible gives a different command:

> And He said to them, "Go into all the world and preach the gospel to every creature" (Mark 16:15).

> Go therefore and make disciples of all the nations, baptizing them in the name of the Father and of the Son and of the Holy Spirit, teaching them to observe all things that I have commanded you; and lo, I am with you always, even to the end of the age (Matt. 28:19–20).

The point is, it is hearts and minds that change a culture. Proverbs 23:7 says clearly of man, "For as he thinks in his heart, so is he."

The secularists certainly understand this. Because the majority of students from church homes are enrolled in the secular education system, these students are being indoctrinated by the world in secular ideas. Churches in the main have concentrated on trying to teach young people the message of Jesus and Christian doctrines — while the education system has been changing their thinking from starting with God's Word to making man's word the starting point. Over time, the student's worldview changes to a secular one, and the more this happens, the more such people cease being light and salt — and the culture changes.

Christians think the battle is with the culture and the moral issues — but ultimately the battle is a foundational one concerning God's Word versus man's word. The majority of Christian leaders, according to our experience and research, have in some way compromised Genesis with the evolutionary/millions of years beliefs of the day — thus contributing toward this change in the foundation of the next generation.[17] This is also why many Christians do not understand the battle because in reality, they have been helping the enemy.

Christians are fighting a war, but they do not know where to fight it or how to aim their guns. This is the real problem. If we want to

---

17. For more on how Christian institutions and leaders are compromising on God's Word, see Ken Ham and Greg Hall, *Already Compromised*, with Britt Beemer (Green Forest, AR: Master Books, 2011).

see the structure of secular humanism collapse (which any thinking Christian must), then we have to re-aim the cannons at the foundation of man's word. It is only when the foundation is destroyed that the structure will collapse. In other words, we need to raise up generations who will stand boldly, unashamedly, and uncompromisingly on the authority of the Word of God. They need to know what they believe and why they believe what they do. They also need to be taught how to defend the Christian faith against the secular attacks of our day (be taught general Bible and creation apologetics). If we were to raise up generations like this, they would be real light and salt, and they would change the world! This second castle diagram illustrates the solution.

Dear reader, there is a war raging. We are soldiers of the King. It is our responsibility to be out there fighting for the King of kings and Lord of lords. We are the King's army. But are we using the right weapons? Are we fighting the battle where it really matters? Unfortunately, many Christians have what would be viewed militarily as a totally ridiculous strategy. They do not fight the battle where it rages. They are not fighting on the real battleground. They have no hope of winning. When are Christians in the nations around the world going to wake up to the fact that we need to re-aim our weapons and aggressively and actively fight the issue at the foundational level?

In Western nations, most churches compromise with evolution and/or millions of years. Many theological and Bible colleges teach that the issue of creation/evolution/age of earth does not matter. They teach that we can believe in evolution and/or millions of years and the Bible, claiming that we do not have to bother about taking Genesis literally. This compromising stand is helping to destroy the very structure they claim to want to remain in society — the structure of Christianity. Chapter 10 challenges all those involved in pastoral and teaching positions in our churches to take a bold stand for God's Word and thus to oppose the anti-God philosophies that are destroying our nations.

CHAPTER 9

EVANGELISM IN
A PAGAN WORLD

THERE IS A WAR GOING ON in society — a very real battle. The war is Christianity versus humanism, but we must wake up to the fact that, at the foundational level, it is God's Word versus man's word. And the attack on God's Word in this era of history is one that is leveled at the first 11 chapters of Genesis.

Having agreed on all this, however, we must remember that our enemies are not the secularists themselves but the powers of darkness that have deceived them:

> But even if our gospel is veiled, it is veiled to those who are perishing, whose minds the god of this age has blinded, who do not believe, lest the light of the gospel of the glory of Christ, who is the image of God, should shine on them (2 Cor. 4:3–4).

We must demonstrate grace toward secularists and those who compromise God's Word with man's beliefs about evolution and millions of years and let them see clearly in us the fruit of the Spirit — in all we say, write, and do.

When Christians understand the foundational nature of the battle, it is a key that unlocks for them the reasons for the happenings in society. It is also a key to unlock an approach to society enabling us to combat its increasingly anti-Christian emphasis and its secularization of the culture and the Church.

It was not so very long ago that God's Word was the basis of our Western society. Even if people were not Christians, most in our Western world had a respect for the Bible and adopted Christian morality. Creation was taught in the universities and the school system. Many people automatically sent their children to Sunday school or similar places so they would learn Christian absolutes. Sexual deviancy in all areas was outlawed. Abortion, in most instances, was considered murder. Gay marriage was not allowed.

But what happened? In this era of history, a particular attack on God's Word (an attack that began in Genesis 3) began to change the way people looked on the Bible. In the late 1700s and 1800s, the belief in millions of years for the fossil-bearing strata began to be popularized. This belief came out of naturalism (atheism).[1] Certain Church leaders then adopted the idea of millions of years and attempted to fit this into the Bible's account of history in Genesis. As a result, some Church leaders promoted the idea of a gap between Genesis 1:1 and Genesis 1:2 to fit in these supposed millions of years (this is appropriately called the gap theory). Others reinterpreted the six days of creation as long periods of time. Some then rejected the global Flood, claiming it was only a local event.

Then in 1859, Charles Darwin, building on this supposed millions of years in geology, applied the idea to biology and claimed that the little changes observed in species were a part of the mechanism for biological evolution. (Actually, there have always been quasi-evolutionary views opposing the true record of creation. Darwin did not originate the idea of evolution; he just popularized a particular version of it.) Evolution was promoted as science. But again, we need to understand the difference between historical and observational science. Darwin's beliefs about evolution are historical science — a belief about the past. Since the time of Darwin, much research has

---

1. For more on the popularization of naturalism, see Terry Mortenson, *The Great Turning Point* (Green Forest, AR: Master Books, 2004).

shown that observational science (e.g., the study of genetics) does not confirm Darwin's ideas but actually contradicts them.

In the midst of the popularization of millions of years and evolution, the Church was caught off guard because it did not know how to handle the situation. Because they did not understand the true nature of science (i.e., that millions of years and molecules-to-man evolution are historical science, not observational science), many people believed that Darwinian evolution and millions of years had to be accepted as fact.

And so this evolutionary view of geological and biological origins began not only to permeate our society but also to permeate the Church. As stated earlier in this book, many in the Church did not think it mattered whether Christians believed in evolution and/or millions of years, as long as they believed the saving gospel of Christ. However, what many Christians did not understand is that while accepting evolutionary ideas and/or millions of years is not a direct attack on Cross, it is an attack on the authority of Word — the Word from which the message of the gospel comes.

As stated in the previous chapter, the clash we see in our society at present is the clash between the religion of Christianity with its creation basis (and therefore absolutes) and the religion of humanism with its evolutionary/millions of years basis and its relative morality that says, "Anything goes." What can we do about it? We must preach the gospel. This means teaching the whole counsel of God to ensure that Jesus Christ is given the glory due His name. But what is the gospel? Many do not really understand the full substance of the gospel. This gospel consists of three major parts:

1. The foundational teachings: Jesus Christ is Creator and He made man; man rebelled against God, and sin therefore entered the world; God placed upon man the Curse of death.

2. The power of the gospel and what is central to the gospel: Jesus Christ, the Creator, came and suffered the same Curse of death on the Cross and was raised from the dead (thus conquering death); all those who come to Him in repentance for their sin (rebellion) can come back to the perfect love relationship with God that was forfeited in the Garden of Eden.

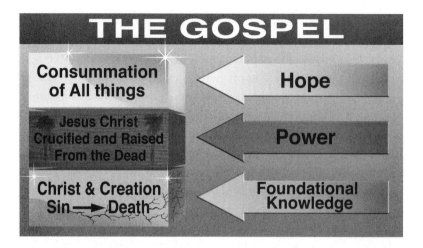

3. The hope of the gospel: The whole of creation is suffering the effects of sin and is slowly running down (Rom. 8:22); all things are to be restored (the consummation of all things) when Jesus Christ comes to complete His work of redemption and reconciliation (Col. 1; 2 Peter 3).

Many people use 1 Corinthians 15 as a passage that defines the gospel and claim that it only talks about Jesus Christ being crucified and raised from the dead. However, in 1 Corinthians 15:12–14 Paul says, "Now if Christ is preached that He has been raised from the dead, how do some among you say that there is no resurrection of the dead? But if there is no resurrection of the dead, then Christ is not risen. And if Christ is not risen, then our preaching is empty and your faith is also empty."

In other words, Paul is talking about the people who do not believe the Resurrection. But now have a look at the tack Paul takes. In verse 21, he goes back to Genesis and explains the origin of sin: "For since by man came death, by Man also came the resurrection of the dead." He sets the foundational reason as to why Jesus Christ came and died on the Cross. It is important to realize that the gospel consists of the foundational aspects as well as the other elements as outlined above. Therefore, to preach the gospel without the message of Christ as Creator and the entrance of sin and death is to preach a gospel without a foundation. To preach a gospel without the message of Christ and His Crucifixion and Resurrection is to preach a gospel without power. To preach a gospel without the message of the coming kingdom is to preach a gospel without hope. All these aspects constitute the gospel. Therefore, to understand the gospel message properly, we must understand all of its aspects.

Even Jesus, upon His appearance to the two on the road to Emmaus, when explaining to them the things concerning Himself (His recent Crucifixion and Resurrection), we read, "And beginning at Moses and all the Prophets, He expounded to them in all the Scriptures the things concerning Himself" (Luke 24:27).

Methods of Evangelism

Many Christians feel that it is sufficient to preach concerning the death of Christ for our sin, the need for repentance, and the receiving of Christ as Savior, leaving the outworking to the Holy Spirit. However, it is quite evident that the early Church evangelists used different presentations according to the people they found before them. Examples abound in Acts and the Gospels:

John 4 — Jesus used the "living water" approach at the well.

Acts 2 — Peter used the explanation of the circumstances of the Day of Pentecost as a starting point.

Acts 3 — Peter used the healing of the lame man to speak of God's power.

Acts 7 — Stephen gave a history lesson to the Sanhedrin.

Acts 13 — Paul preached Jesus as the Christ in the synagogue.

Acts 14 and 17 — Paul preached the *Creator God* to the Gentiles.

The Lord has raised up biblical creation organizations worldwide so that all necessary methods for evangelizing our society will be available. The Lord has provided us with a phenomenally powerful tool that needs to be used today: *creation evangelism*. The main reason, we believe, that the Church is so relatively ineffective is a direct result of not understanding the real state of today's culture and therefore not evangelizing correctly. The Church is proclaiming the message of the Cross and Christ, but it is not as effective as it used to be. We also read in the New Testament (1 Cor. 1:23) that the preaching of the Cross was foolishness to the Gentiles (Greeks) but only a stumbling block to the Jews. We need to take a lesson from the New Testament. In Acts 14 and 17, we are given two specific approaches to the Greeks. It was a different method from that used for the Jews. When Paul went to the Greeks, he did not start preaching about Jesus Christ and the Cross. The Greeks believed in a form of evolution in a culture that had many temples and many gods. In their eyes, there was no one Creator God who had authority over them.

There are only two types of views about origins: evolutionary or creationist. If one does not believe that there is an infinite being who created all, the only alternative is that some form of evolution must apply.

When we think about this very carefully, we can begin to understand why Paul needed to approach the Greeks on the basis of creation. The Greeks, who did not believe in God as Creator but rather believed in a form of evolution (and had no concept of the origin of sin because they did not have or believe the writings of Moses concerning Adam and Eve), had the wrong basis and therefore, the wrong framework of thinking about this world. Consequently, to them the preaching of the Cross was utter foolishness. Paul realized that before he could preach about Jesus Christ, he had to establish the basis upon which he could build the rest of the gospel. So he established creation as a foundation, explained they were all "one blood" (laying down the history that is foundational to the gospel), and from there preached the message of Jesus Christ.

Whenever the Jews were approached, it was not with the message of creation first but the teaching of Christ and the Cross (e.g., Peter on the day of Pentecost in Acts 2). The Jews (at that time in history)

already had the right foundation because they believed in God as Creator; they believed in the account of Adam and Eve and the Fall; they understood the meaning of the first sacrifice and why they had the sacrificial system; therefore, they had the right foundational history to understand the gospel. However, their stumbling block was that Jesus was the Messiah (1 Cor. 1:23).

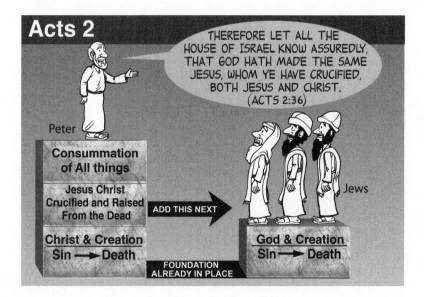

It is about time the modern Church came to grips with a society that is more Greek than Jewish in outlook (to use the terms *Greek* and *Jew* as types). In fact, the modern Church itself is largely more Greek than Jewish. Or to put it another way, our Western culture used to be more like Acts 2, where most people knew about or believed the history in Genesis concerning Adam and Eve and the entrance of sin. However, the Western world has become much more like Acts 17, with generations who no longer believe the account of history in Genesis.

In an Acts 2 culture (one that is more Jewish), one could preach the message of sin, of the Crucifixion and the Resurrection, and of our need for repentance, and people would understand — and even respond by committing their lives to the Lord.

In an Acts 17 culture (one that is more Greek), the preaching of the message of sin and of the Crucifixion and the Resurrection is really not understood. Such a culture needs the presentation of the gospel the way God does it in the Bible — by starting at the beginning! And in this era of history, as well as presenting the gospel by starting at the beginning, there also needs to be apologetic teaching to answer the skeptical questions of the age and to deal with the evolutionary/millions of years indoctrination that has caused so many to reject the Bible's history as true. Because people do not believe the history is true, they will not listen to the gospel based in that history.

In the past, the biblical basis was evident in society, and people were less ignorant of Christian doctrine, but late 20th- and early 21st-century man knows little of that. We have to come to grips with the fact that evolution and millions of years have become major barriers to people today being receptive to the gospel of Jesus Christ. We have received many letters, emails, and phone calls from people over the years testifying that they would not listen to the claims of Christianity because they thought evolution and millions of years had proved the Bible to be untrustworthy.

We must appreciate that there are whole generations of students coming through an educational system who know very little of the Bible. Increasingly, there are many who have never heard about creation, the Fall of man, or Noah's Flood. They do not understand the foundational history, and so they do not understand the gospel based in that history. It is hard to believe that there are literally millions of people in Western society who do not have this background, but it is becoming increasingly obvious.

In an increasing number of instances, it is apparent that before we can effectively proclaim the message of Christ we must establish the creation/Fall foundation upon which the rest of the gospel can be built.

Let me be emphatic here. The doctrine of the Cross, though regarded as absurd and powerless by non-Christians, has more power and wisdom than anything that ever proceeded from man. The preaching of this doctrine is the great means of salvation. To this, all other teachings, however important, are either preparatory or subordinate. The doctrine of Christ crucified produces effects that nothing short of divine power can accomplish. So, in saying that we need to start from the foundational basis of creation, I am not detracting from the message of the Cross. What I am attempting to show is that there is a particular method of approach that is necessary when presenting the gospel message to certain people. The beliefs that they hold can be barriers to their even listening to or understanding the message of the Cross.

Perhaps, too, we should rethink the method prevalent in Christian circles of handing unbelievers numerous copies of the New Testament, Psalms, and Proverbs. If they were directed to Genesis 1 through 11 (along with some answers to skeptical questions that cause them to doubt God's Word in this era of history), as well as the New Testament, the basis would be provided for the gospel presentation in the same sense as Paul used it in Acts 14 and 17. We believe there would be greater effectiveness in the lives of those who read these Bible portions — a greater preparedness to accept the whole of the Word of God as truthful and inerrant.

And really, when you think about it, the Bible is for all people, for all time, and stands for eternity. And how does God present the gospel in His Word? He starts at the beginning — with Genesis! Surely then we should use this approach with all people. But I am also saying, in understanding 21st-century man, we know that the teaching of evolution and millions of years has been used to attack God's Word in Genesis — evolutionary ideas create doubt and unbelief concerning the Word of God. That is why, in this era of history, we need to use creation apologetics to deal with the barriers that cause people to doubt and disbelieve God's Word in Genesis, so they will understand that the history in the Bible is true, and therefore the gospel based in that history is true.

Evolution as a barrier can also be seen in Islamic countries. On one occasion, I was speaking to a Christian Egyptian who told me that Islam is a creation-based religion, but the teaching of evolution in schools in Egypt caused many young people to totally reject this religion. It is interesting to see that another creation-based religion (though a false one) has the same problem with evolution. This should make it even more obvious to Christians that evolution/millions of years is a barrier to people's believing in a Creator God.

I have seen this problem in the public school system. Students would often say such things as, "Sir, how can you believe the Bible is true when it says God created Adam and Eve? We know that has been proved wrong by science." Evolution and millions of years, I believe, are some of the biggest barriers to people today being receptive to the gospel of Jesus Christ. Many people (who previously would not consider Christianity) have come to listen to the message of Christianity after these barriers were removed.

For example, a high school student in Nevada wrote about how creation apologetics affected him:

> I just wanted to let you know that I just got saved! I'm so excited about my new faith! I go to a Christian high school, and in my Christian studies class, my teacher showed us some Ken Ham videos. I was so amazed at all the evidence he put forth for the existence of God, and the fact that Jesus came to die on the cross for our sins. Part of me still remained skeptical, and a few days later (today), I battled it all out in my mind. I finally received Jesus Christ as my Lord and Savior, and I'm so glad that Answers in Genesis was here for the important questions of the Christian faith that I needed answered. It seems that the mainstream Christian churches today all teach from the New Testament only, and they don't have answers for questions that are critical for the foundation of Christianity. So, I just wanted to thank everyone at AIG, and Ken Ham, for opening my eyes to Christianity!

This was creation apologetics at work! I have heard this kind of testimony many, many times during my years in the creation evangelism ministry.

If God's people do not take up the tool of creation evangelism and use it, we will suffer the consequences of an ineffective method of proclaiming the truth. This is why biblical creation organizations are so important today. They deal with the foundations upon which Christianity depends — the foundations that have been removed to a great extent from our society.

As this message has been preached throughout Australia, the United States, and other places around the world, we have seen people take the apologetics teaching and publications and challenge others in the area of origins. When confronted on that issue, they have been found to be open to the gospel, whereas previously they would simply scoff when the subject of Christ was raised. By the grace of God, creation evangelism works!

More and more mission organizations (like New Tribes Mission) are also recognizing that when presenting the gospel to a pagan group of people, it is much more effective to begin teaching chronologically through the Bible, starting with Genesis.[2] Then, when they get to the message of the Cross, the people understand the gospel — and respond.

When new converts come into a church, they should be led in a Bible study on the Book of Genesis. They will learn exactly what Christianity is all about and will learn the basis for all Christian doctrine. Results do come from simply preaching about Christ and the Cross in our society today because there is still a remnant of Acts 2-type people who respond to that kind of preaching. But this remnant is disappearing very quickly, and thus the response is far less today than in the past. It is time we woke up and used the tools that the Lord has provided to evangelize a society that has become like the ancient Greeks. It is time to restore the foundations of Christianity.

A good example of creation evangelism at work can be summarized in the letter we received from an excited young university student:

2. For an example of evangelizing chronologically, see *Ee-taow!* DVD, directed by John R. Cross (Sanford, FL: New Tribes Mission, 1999).

I would like to thank you for your ministry as you help people understand that Jesus actually created this world.

I want to share a testimony that I pray will encourage you in your fight against evolution.

My father for 65 years had been an atheist. He always had been an atheist and was always quick to knock down anyone's beliefs concerning God in general, but especially if they claimed that God had made the world. Dad thought the Bible was illogical and a book for the simple in mind. "How could it contain any truth?" he questioned. Dad assumed that evolution was the only possible scientific way to explain the formation of the earth.

Sensing this spiritual attack, my faithful mother prayed for twenty years for Dad's mind to open to the truth and for this deception to be broken. Two years ago, when I was eighteen and had been a Christian for three years, I decided to go to a creation science seminar. I can't tell you how impressed I was with these Bible-believing Christians presenting scientific truth about creation. It made my faith in God's Word increasingly stronger, and I was overjoyed that I could take a scientific stand to explain how God created the world.

At the bookstand at the seminar, I bought several books and magazines. One in particular was *Bone of Contention*. I loved reading this magazine so much that I encouraged Dad to read it. Skeptically, he took it and started reading it. Three days after, I asked him what he thought about it. To my surprise he stated that it really made him think. At this opening, I then proceeded to give him the other books I had bought.

A few weeks later Dad was making statements like "never knew there were so many holes in the evolutionary theory. There must have been an Almighty Being who created the world." Each new day Jesus began to piece together the puzzle in Dad's mind concerning creation and the claim of Jesus on his life. A few weeks later, an evangelist came to our church. The same night Dad decided to go. The evangelist spoke on creation versus evolution. God's timing is perfect! That night Dad accepted Jesus Christ into his heart as his personal Savior!

I praise God that He can take a lost soul off the highway to hell and set him on the path to life simply because an understanding of how God created the world was formed in his mind!

Thanks . . . for teaching people about creation. I want to encourage you in your fight against Satan. The Lord is doing wonderful things as a result of your effort.

That letter was written over 25 years ago, and we continue to receive such responses today — but in greater volume as the biblical creation ministry has grown and had a great effect on Church and culture. The growing need for creation apologetics is evidenced by this testimony from a reader of *Answers* magazine, a quarterly magazine published by Answers in Genesis:

I'm the fourth- and fifth-grade coordinator at [our church]. We have been using New Tribes' "Firm Foundations: Creation to Christ" for almost two years now. The results are priceless. From the time I began college, I have questioned the way the Church is generally presenting the gospel today. In reality, the simple tracts, presenting only the death, burial, and Resurrection of our Savior, are not having as great of an impact as they once had. I believe that one of the reasons for this is the biblical illiteracy that dominates our society. When tracts were originally handed out, they were given to people who had some Bible background; but today, people with even minimal Bible knowledge are difficult to find. Unfortunately, this biblical illiteracy is also found in the Church — much more than most people would like to admit. Since we have started using the creation evangelism approach, both our children, and their parents have grown in their knowledge of the Scriptures. They understand the Bible to be one continual story, with one outstanding purpose — the message of redemption through Christ alone! It is when this outstanding purpose is revealed, and the dots are connected throughout Scripture, that the lights go off, and a biblical understanding of redemption takes place. I've also seen this work with neighbors, and children at the YMCA. I believe creation evangelism to be, in most cases, a necessity.

Creation evangelism is *a necessity!* This teacher has seen the fruit of starting at the beginning when sharing the gospel in today's culture — which is exactly the tack we take at the Creation Museum. Recently, an AiG staff member shared the testimony of a family who visited the Creation Museum and called later to share their news:

> A family was visiting their brother and sister-in-law for Thanksgiving and wanted to come to the museum; they tried to convince their extended family to come with them, but they declined. So they came the Friday after Thanksgiving and went through the entire museum, ending with the Last Adam show. At the end of the show, her six-year-old son . . . grabbed one of the cards (credit card type, the one you can sign the back of if you make a commitment to Christ) and took it home. Later that night, as he was drying off from his bath, he turned and looked at his mom and asked, "Mommy, am I a Christian?" So they talked and prayed because he really wanted to know Jesus. He was so happy after that while he was brushing his teeth, he kept stopping to sing, "I'm a Christian, I'm a Christian!" They went and told his dad then pulled out that little card and he proudly signed his name and dated the card. It is now stored in his memory drawer.

What a blessing to hear about a child committing his life to the Lord as a result of visiting the museum. But creation evangelism reaches more than children. A former atheist emailed me his testimony in 2010:

> When I was in junior high school, our teacher taught us evolution as fact. We were all lined up side by side in our desks, each with the same hardcover book with glossy pages, paid for by the U.S. government we were told we could trust to tell us the truth.
>
> We were indoctrinated into believing whatever the teachers told us was gospel truth. They were the educators; they were the ones we were trained to expect had answers. So when our teacher told us life originated by a single cell coming to life on its own and that it had then evolved into all the life

on this earth, time seemed to stop for me. I immediately realized that this meant science had disproved the Bible. Life and death had no meaning; everything was merely the result of natural physical processes. I lost my [trust] in Jesus Christ.

I was an atheist for ten years, but by the grace of God, I was given Answers in Genesis videos after that decade of darkness. As I watched Ken Ham give biblical answers to evolution, I realized how the atheist/public education system in America had brainwashed me.

I adamantly bought and read books and magazines from AiG, and especially enjoyed the DVD lectures. I am now a passionate Christian in love with my Lord and Savior Jesus Christ, and I can't wait to thank Ken Ham and the rest of the Answers in Genesis staff for all they've done to help make my relationship with Jesus happen.

God bless your biblical work for the Lord Jesus!

— J. B.

That testimony is a great example of how creation evangelism can remove the barriers to salvation for people. The Lord has not just called us to tear down the barriers of evolution and millions of years but also to help to restore the foundation of the gospel in our society. If churches took up the tool of creation evangelism (with creation apologetics) in both the culture and the Church, we would see a stemming of the tide of secularism and of the exodus of young people from the Church.

In Australia's Christian newspaper, *New Life*, Thursday, April 15, 1982, Josef Ton, who was a pastor of the largest Baptist church in Romania and is now living in exile in the United States, stated: "I came to the conclusion that there were two factors which destroyed Christianity in Western Europe. One was the theory of evolution, and the other, liberal theology. . . . Liberal theology is just evolution applied to the Bible and our faith."

It is also worth noting the comment in the book *By Their Blood: Christian Martyrs of the 20th Century*, by James and Marti Hefley:

New philosophies and theologies from the West also helped to erode Chinese confidence in Christianity. A new wave of so-called missionaries from mainline Protestant denominations came teaching evolution and a non-super-natural view of the Bible. Methodist, Presbyterian, Congregational, and Northern Baptist schools were especially hard hit. Bertrand Russell came from England preaching atheism and socialism. Destructive books brought by such teachers further undermined orthodox Christianity. *The Chinese intelligentsia who had been schooled by orthodox evangelical missionaries were thus softened for the advent of Marxism* [emphasis mine]. Evolution is destroying the Church and society today, and Christians need to be awakened to that fact.[3]

Sowing and Reaping

Think about the parable of the sower of the seed (Matt. 13:3–23). When the seed fell on rocky and thorny ground, it could not grow. It only grew when it fell on prepared ground. We throw the seed out that represents the gospel. It is falling on the thorny ground and rocky ground of millions of years and evolutionary beliefs. The gospel needs prepared ground. Creation evangelism enables us to prepare the ground so the good seed can be scattered and a great harvest reaped. Imagine what would happen if our churches really stood up for God's Word beginning in Genesis in our society! Creation evangelism is one of the means whereby we could see revival.

---

3. James and Marti Hefley, *By Their Blood: Christian Martyrs of the 20th Century* (Milford, MI: Mott Media, 1979), p. 49–50.

We are not suggesting that a true revival can be engineered by simply adopting certain clever human strategies. Revival is essentially the sovereign work of God pouring out His Spirit. But the history of the Church suggests that God's movement in this area is related to the faithful prayer of His people and to the faithful preaching of the gospel, giving due honor to God and His Word. Note the nature of the "everlasting gospel" preached by the angel in Revelation 14:7: "Fear God and give glory to Him, for the hour of His judgment has come; and worship Him who made heaven and earth, the sea and springs of water." Can the Body of Christ really expect a great outpouring of God's Spirit in revival while we tolerate and compromise with a religious system (evolution/millions of years) that was set up primarily to deny God the glory and worship due to Him as the great Creator, Judge, and Redeemer?

As a result of the biblical creation apologetics ministry, many people who previously would not listen to the gospel have realized that evolution/millions of years are not proven scientific fact. They have heard the message of creation, the Fall, and redemption, and they have committed their lives to our Lord Jesus Christ. Large numbers of Christians have testified that their faith in the Scriptures has been restored. Instead of coming to the Bible with doubts, they know that it really is the Word of God. They can share the facts of Christianity with their neighbors and friends without wondering whether the Bible can be trusted. Christians have also had their eyes opened to the truth that to comprehend Christianity they have to understand the foundational Book of Genesis. When Christians have been equipped with answers to the skeptical questions of our day that are aimed at God's Word in Genesis, they are no longer intimidated and will boldly stand on the authority of the Word, answer the questions, and proclaim the gospel.

After hearing me preach on this particular topic, a minister at one church informed his congregation that he had not realized before what he had been doing in his ministry in attempting to combat secular philosophy. He was, as it were, "cutting the tops off the weeds." The weeds kept growing back bigger and better than before. After listening to the message on creation evangelism, he realized this was simply not good enough. He had to remove the pestilence, roots and all. The biblical creation ministry is a plowing ministry: plowing up the ground, getting rid of the barriers of evolution and millions of years (getting rid of the weeds), and preparing the ground for the seed to be planted.

In thinking about the idea I presented earlier, that our culture is more Greek than Jewish, I like to call the biblical creation ministry such as that of Answers in Genesis a "de-Greekizing" ministry![4] God's people today need to be "de-Greekizing" people's thinking, so that they will understand and be receptive to the teaching of God's Word and the gospel.

---

4. Yes, I made up this word to get people's attention. The Church and culture has been what I call "Greekized," so we need to "de-Greekize." That is what preparing the ground is all about.

CHAPTER 10

WAKE UP, SHEPHERDS!

MUCH OPPOSITION TO biblical creation ministry comes from within the Church, particularly from those who have compromised God's Word with evolutionary ideas and/or millions of years. First, please understand that I do not want to sound as if I am hitting too hard at those who have done this. Many people simply do not understand the real issues involved. They really believe scientists have proven evolutionary ideas. For many people, a belief in such positions as theistic evolution, the gap theory, day-age theory, progressive creation, and the many other positions on Genesis that are rife in the Church came out of sheer pressure from their belief that not to believe in evolution and/or millions of years is to reject science. However, we dealt with this in previous chapters. I simply want to remind you that there is a vast difference between historical science and observational science. The origins battle is really one over two different accounts of historical science (i.e., beliefs about the past).

At one seminar, a lady told me that evolutionary beliefs had destroyed her faith in the Scriptures. She had such emptiness in her life that she cried to the Lord and prayed for a solution to this problem.

She was finding it impossible to trust the Scriptures. She was led to a library and happened to find a book on the gap theory, which basically allows for billions of years between Genesis 1:1 and Genesis 1:2. (For further explanation, see appendix 3.) She was thrilled at this explanation and set about rebuilding her Christian life. At the end of the seminar, however, she came to me and exclaimed what a thrill it was to know she did not have to believe the gap theory. She did say, though, that the Lord used the gap theory to bring her out of a situation that was caused by the belief in evolution and millions of years. Now she could totally trust the Bible.

There have been many great Christian men and women in past generations who promoted the gap theory, theistic evolution, or other compromise positions on Genesis. However, now that we can show the powerful evidence supporting the Bible in every area, there is no need to cling to these positions of compromise. Not only is there no need, but it is imperative that Christians give up these positions and accept the Bible as the authoritative Word of God. In fact, that should be our position even if we did not have all the answers we have today.

James 3:1 warns us, "My brethren, let not many of you become teachers, knowing that we shall receive a stricter judgment."

I am appealing to all Christian leaders to consider seriously their beliefs about the question of origins and the age of the earth. After I spoke at one school, I received the testimony of a young student from that school, in which he shared the resultant openness of the students to the gospel message. One of the difficulties of speaking there, however, was the virulent opposition of two ministers from that district who tried to bar my entrance to the school. Their reason? They said I would only confuse the students. They indicated that I had no right to insist that the biblical account of creation be taken literally. If they had been successful in their endeavor, many of those students would not now be open to the gospel.

At another school, one of the local ministers spent a great deal of time obtaining special permission for the creation apologists team to speak to some of the classes. Another local minister went to the school and demanded the right to speak after we had spoken. He told the students that he was a Christian and a minister of religion, and then he appealed to them not to believe what we were saying. He said he believed in evolution and did not believe Genesis was true.

Such events have occurred many times during my experience as an apologetics speaker dealing with the biblical and scientific aspects of creation. Again and again, we hear Christian leaders claim that we would only confuse students and so should not be allowed into schools. These Christian leaders are oblivious to the fact that students are being told there is no God and everything (including man) is a result of random chance over billions of years. They are being told that man is just an animal — just another ape. Our message is simple. We are telling the students there is a God, that He is Creator, and that the Bible can be trusted from the very first verse. How can men, who are supposed to be caring pastors, prefer that students be told that the Bible's history is not true — that the bottom line is that there is no God and everything came about by natural processes? These men have no faith in their own pilgrimage. How can they ever hope to shepherd others? They should actually visit the school and ask the students what the teaching of evolutionism (cosmological evolution, geological evolution, and biological evolution) is doing to them.

In one church school in Tasmania, Australia, the official position was to teach evolution with God added to it. The local bishop tried his hardest to prevent my visit to the school, but one of the teachers was allowed to present the creationist position to the class, and he invited me as a special speaker. At the conclusion of my presentation, 69 of the 70 girls surrounded me and verbally attacked my stand on creation. They shouted statements such as: "There is no God!" "Buddhism is better than Christianity!" "Evolution is true!" "You can't trust the Bible!" "The Bible is full of mistakes!" "We are not interested in what you have to say."

Because of the compromise with evolution and millions of years, they were even less open to God's Word than public school students. They attended a "church" school. Why wouldn't they know the truth? As far as they were concerned, they already had all the answers. One young girl, however, came to me with tears in her eyes. She thanked me for the foundation given her faith. She said she was a Bible-believing Christian and that she found it very hard to be in that particular school because the teachers were attempting to destroy her faith in Christianity. They had obviously weakened the faith of many of the other girls in the class.

During a question time at one church, the minister raised a vital question. Because there was no Christian school in the district that taught from the creationist perspective, should parents be advised to send their children to the local public school with its known anti-Christian philosophy or to the compromising Christian school in the area? There was silence as the congregation awaited my answer.

What was my answer? Send their children to a church school that compromised with evolution and only taught a secular philosophy, or send them to the local public school? My first answer was, "I would send them to neither; I would keep them home!" Of course, this is becoming a real option for many parents today, and the homeschool movement is growing in many countries. However, I did go on to add that it was easier in one sense to tell the students they were being taught an anti-Christian philosophy in the public school. A church school that is supposedly Christian but has compromised with secular philosophy is no different from the public schools, except that it purports to be Christian. To me, this is a huge problem.

The Lord makes this clear to us in Revelation 3:15–16. In reference to the compromising Church, we read, "I know your works, that you are neither cold nor hot. I could wish you were cold or hot. So then, because you are lukewarm, and neither cold nor hot, I will vomit you out of My mouth."

Pastors! Theologians! Ministers! You must be aware of what the teaching of evolution and millions of years is doing to students' minds. You must be aware of what is happening in the school system. Remember the *Already Gone* research.[1] Two-thirds of young people are leaving the Church by the time they reach college age — and the major contributing factors have been compromised teaching on Genesis and the lack of teaching on apologetics to defend the Christian faith and God's Word in Genesis. Look at it practically. Is the compromise position working? It is not! We are losing the culture in America

1. Ken Ham and Britt Beemer, *Already Gone: Why Your Kids Will Quit Church and What You Can Do to Stop It*, with Todd Hillard (Green Forest, AR: Master Books, 2009).

and other nations that were once very Christianized. Look at how pagan England is today. That is where America is heading — and for the same basic reason. Most of the Church and its leaders have adopted the pagan religion of the day (evolution/millions of years) and compromised on God's Word.

Some of the opposition we encounter could be seen in the interview on Australian radio on May 16, 1984, with the Reverend Colin Honey, a Uniting Church minister and master of Kingswood College at the University of Western Australia. Reverend Honey was asked if he saw a fundamental confusion between Christianity and simple-mindedness. He replied, "I guess there will be in people's minds, if fools keep telling us that the Bible says the world was created in six days."

In 2002, Pat Robertson on *The 700 Club* asked his co-host, Terry Meeuwson, if she would align herself with a belief in a literal creation week. Meeuwson indicated that she would not, and Robertson agreed, explaining his reasons:

> I'm with you, I couldn't either because, you know, we could be looking at a solar day; we could be looking at a universal day; we could be looking at a galactic day. It doesn't have to be one revolution of the earth. And I mean, [as] you say, "nobody was there." . . . Genesis was never intended as a science textbook. Genesis is the backdrop for the introduction of the Jewish race through Abraham, which was God's agency of salvation through Jesus Christ. That's what Genesis is all about.[2]

You would be in for a shock if you wrote to or visited some of our theological or Bible colleges and asked them what they teach about creation. Actually, we have already done that for you. The results are published in the book entitled *Already Compromised*, which, as I said in a prior chapter, came about from the study America's Research Group conducted with us.[3] Sadly, we found the majority of professors at such institutions compromise Genesis in some way. In fact,

---

2. Pat Robertson and Terry Meeuwson, *The 700 Club*, CBN, June 17, 2002.
3. Ken Ham and Greg Hall, *Already Compromised*, with Britt Beemer (Green Forest, AR: Master Books, 2011).

by and large, we found the Bible/religion departments were worse than the science departments.

But if you do ask the leaders of such institutions what they teach about Genesis, be very specific; do not just ask them if they teach creation. Ask them what they believe about Genesis. Do they believe the days were real days? Do they believe the Flood of Noah was worldwide in extent? Do they take Genesis literally? Do they see the importance of Genesis to doctrine?

I have often said to people in churches that I knew the theological college of that particular denomination either taught evolution or the view that Genesis does not matter. Most people reel in shock. They had believed their theological colleges taught that the Bible is true in Genesis. *One of the problems we have in the West is that most theological and Bible colleges produce ministers who have been trained to question the Scriptures rather than accept them. That is why we have so many shepherds in our churches who are really leading the sheep astray.* If you support any of these institutions financially, why not ask them what they teach about these matters? I would also urge you to read *Already Compromised*. It is eye opening and may change where you send your son or daughter for college — which may be a vital change that is needed for the future.

At one seminar, three ministers from a Protestant denomination came up to me. They said that what I was teaching was a perversion of the Scriptures. As we talked, it became obvious that we were arguing from two totally different approaches to the Scripture. I asked these people how God made the first woman. I said the Bible claims that God took a rib from Adam's side and made a woman — did they believe that? Their answer went something like this: "Yes, we do believe the symbolic picture implied here that men and women are one."

"No," I said, "I asked you whether you believed that that is how God actually made a woman." They said they certainly agreed that this theological picture implied that men and women are one. I repeated my question a number of times, saying that the Bible claims this is actually how God made a woman. Not only that, but in the New Testament in 1 Corinthians 11:8, Paul states that the woman came from the man and not the man from the woman, obviously supporting the historical creation account in Genesis.

We were getting nowhere, so I asked them if they believed that Jesus was nailed on a Cross as the New Testament states. "Oh, yes," they said, "we certainly believe that." I then asked them why they did not believe God actually took a rib from Adam's side and made a woman. They told me it was the difference between accepting Genesis as poetry rather than history, suggesting that if it were poetry it should not be believed.

Genesis, of course, is history. It is written in the typical style of a Hebrew historical narrative. And besides, even if something is written in poetic form, as indeed other parts of the Scriptures are (like the Psalms), does this then indicate that we should not believe it?

They informed me that, for much of Scripture, it was not what was said that was important but the theological picture that was implied. I asked them how they determined what that theological picture was, on what basis did they decide what was the true theological picture, and how could they be sure that their approach to Scripture was the right one? From where did they obtain their authority to approach the Scripture this way? They said it was their study of history and theology over the years that enabled them to decide what was the correct way to approach Scripture and to determine what these symbolic pictures were. I then told them it sounded as though they simply held an opinion as to how to approach Scripture. How did they know it was the right opinion? This is where the conversation abruptly ended. These men want to tell God what He is saying rather than letting God tell them what the truth is. This is the position of many theological leaders today.

After I spoke at a church in Victoria, Australia, one of the local pastors (who was obviously upset) told me in front of a large number of people that I had no right to force my interpretation of the Bible on others. He was extremely vocal and emotional about this issue. The thing I found amazing was that he was trying to force his interpretation of the Bible on me and the others who were present. He could not comprehend that aspect.

There are many passages throughout the Bible in which God rebukes religious leaders for leading people astray. Jeremiah, for instance, was called by the Lord to warn the Israelites about teachers and priests who were not proclaiming the truth. Jesus openly rebuked many religious leaders, calling them such names as "vipers" (Matt. 12:34).

These same warnings apply to many today who claim to be teachers of the Word of God, but who, in reality, are causing many people to fall by the wayside. Many of you will no doubt be aware that much of the opposition to the work of the biblical creation organizations worldwide comes from theologians and other religious leaders. Many of the secular humanist groups often enlist people who profess to be Christians but who also believe in evolution and millions of years to support them (on television, on the radio, and in publications) in their effort to combat the biblical creation movement. I have seen TV reporters and radio announcers reveling in the fact that they can have someone on their program who claims to be a Christian but who opposes the Bible's account of origins in Genesis.

At one creation-versus-evolution debate, an evolutionist stated that the issue was not whether God created. He said that he believed in creation and that he was a Christian. He then went on to vehemently attack the Bible and Christianity. During the question time, someone in the audience asked this person whether he could testify to Jesus Christ being his personal Savior. The evolutionist debater, caught off guard, obviously wanted to avoid the question. However, he decided to attempt an answer. He told the audience he did not use the same terminology as others and that he certainly did not accept the Bible at all and would not have anything to do with fundamental Christianity. Basically, he described fundamental Christianity as the belief that accepted the Bible as true. Yet, many probably had believed that he was a Christian because he publicly stated so. Here was a wolf in sheep's clothing leading sheep astray.

Many shepherds of the sheep in today's world can be found in one of the following groups, in the sliding progression from toleration to capitulation to error.

1. Toleration

Many tell us we should tolerate other people's beliefs about evolution — that we must refrain from speaking against what they say. Or we are told to consider all alternatives that scientists put before us and not to be dogmatic about one view. Of course, this is a form of dogmatism itself, claiming that we cannot insist Genesis be taken literally so as to exclude evolutionary beliefs. Many theological colleges dogmatically insist that students consider all views on the interpretation of Genesis (e.g., theistic evolution, progressive creation, the day-age theory, the gap theory, six-day literal creation, and others) and go on to assert that no one person may say that any view is definitely correct or incorrect. I am not suggesting that students at such colleges should not be made aware of these other positions. However, the fallacies of the positions that compromise with man's ideas should be pointed out in detail.

2. Accommodation

Many are saying that you cannot be sure what Genesis means or says and perhaps that evolutionists are right after all. Because of the high respect for academia and the immense amount of material from a large number of scientists pushing evolutionary ideas, many Christians just add evolutionary ideas to the Bible.

3. Cooperation

Here the errors of evolution and/or millions of years have been tolerated and given standing in the Church. This has become a comfortable position because there is great harmony: the people in the Church who believe in evolution and/or millions of years do not feel threatened, and they can all work together. Such people claim that God created, but whether He worked through evolution and/or millions of years, it does not really matter.

4. Contamination

With people becoming so intimately involved with the error of evolutionary ideas (in cosmology, geology, and biology), these then become generally accepted and taught through the churches, Sunday schools, Christian schools, and religious educational programs, as well as in the secular school classrooms. Consequently, the issue does not bother people anymore.

5. Capitulation to Error

Evolution and/or millions of years become accepted as fact, and anyone who dares to disagree is a heretic. Because people then relegate Genesis to myth or allegory, they start to question the rest of Scripture. A rejection of the foundations of all doctrine contained in the book of Genesis logically leads one to a denial of the entire Bible. Liberal theology becomes rampant. Doubt leads to a slippery slide of unbelief through Scripture.

It was interesting to note the reaction of a professor in genetics and human variation at the School of Biological Science at LaTrobe University. When he was asked a question during a debate with Dr. Gary Parker relating to the fact that many Christians do accept evolution, he stated, "I can only add that Christianity is fairly widely fragmented. Obviously, Christianity is in various stages of evolution; some sections of it seem to have just about dispensed with the theology altogether. It seems to be that the ultimate stage of evolutionary Christianity will be to just throw out all the theology and be left with an entirely rational and naturalistic system of outlook on life." What he recognized, of course, was that there is really no difference between atheistic and theistic evolution — except that in the latter God is added to the system. Logically, therefore, theistic evolution is only one step away from atheistic evolution, and that is where he sees the ultimate end of such a compromise situation.

Richard Dawkins has basically said much the same. In two different television interviews, he expressed the sentiment that a belief in God and a belief in evolutionary ideas are not compatible. When asked about whether one could believe in God and evolution, Dawkins had this to say:

> Obviously you can be a believer in God and in evolution . . . I find it slightly hard. I have a certain niggling sympathy for the creationist because I think, in a way, the writing is on the wall for the religious few that says it's fully compatible with evolution. I think there's a kind of incompatibility which the creationists see clearly.[4]

What he is saying is that he agrees with those in the Church who believe in evolution, but he sees that as being incompatible

---

4. Richard Dawkins, interview by Tony Jones, *Q&A: Adventures in Democracy*, ABC1 (Australia), March 8, 2010, http://www.abc.net.au/tv/qanda/txt/s2831712.htm.

with Genesis. Thus, the writing is on the wall means that he sees the only solution is for those who try to mix evolution with the Bible to totally throw out the Bible.

In an interview that has since been pulled from the web, Richard Dawkins once again pointed out the incompatibility of Christianity and evolutionary beliefs:

> I think the evangelical Christians have really sort of got it right in a way in seeing evolution as the enemy. Whereas the more, what shall we say, sophisticated theologians are quite happy to live with evolution. I think they're deluded. I think the evangelicals have got it right in that there really is a deep incompatibility between evolution and Christianity.[5]

In many denominations, there is real controversy and a lot of discussion concerning inerrancy of the Bible. When discussing this issue, the sad thing is that many evangelical scholars do not recognize or deliberately sidestep the importance of Genesis. The acceptance of the literal events in Genesis is foundational to the question of biblical inerrancy. If the conferences on inerrancy were to settle that issue first, the rest of the problems they have would disappear very quickly.

This is another reason why any statement of faith being formulated for Christian schools, Christian organizations, churches, and such conferences should always be very specific concerning Genesis. It is not good enough to say that they believe God created. They need to understand the importance and relevance of accepting Genesis literally, of rejecting evolution and millions of years completely, and of understanding the foundational nature of Genesis to the rest of the Bible.

Unfortunately, even much of the Christian school movement is devoid of this understanding. I know of Christian schools that are more concerned with their teacher's view of eschatology (the Second Coming) than with what they believe and understand concerning the foundational issue of creation. This means they do not fully understand Christian education!

As the prophet Hosea says, "Therefore people who do not understand will be trampled" (Hosea 4:14). While there are many

---

5. Richard Dawkins, interview with Howard Condor, *The Q&A Show*, RevelationTV (UK), March 10, 2011.

shepherds leading the sheep astray, we must remember that the sheep are also to blame, as God tells us through Jeremiah 5:31: "The prophets prophesy falsely, And the priests rule by their own power; And My people love *to have it so*" (emphasis mine). Let us pray that more men and women in our nations will be prepared to stand for the absolute truth of God's Holy Word from the very first verse.

Exodus 20:11 states, "For in six days the LORD made the heavens and the earth, the sea, and all that is in them, and rested the seventh day. Therefore the LORD blessed the Sabbath day and hallowed it."

A child in a Christian school class asked her teacher, "How could anybody create everything in six days from nothing?" Another very discerning young student blurted out, "But God is not just *anybody!*"

CHAPTER 11

CREATION, FLOOD, AND COMING FIRE

THERE IS A PROPHECY in 2 Peter 3 concerning the last days of this earth's history, and it very much relates to the whole creation/evolution issue:

> Knowing this first: that scoffers will come in the last days, walking according to their own lusts, and saying, "Where is the promise of His coming? For since the fathers fell asleep, all things continue as they were from the beginning of creation." For this they willfully forget: that by the word of God the heavens were of old, and the earth standing out of water and in the water, by which the world that then existed perished, being flooded with water. But the heavens and the earth which are now preserved by the same word, are reserved for fire until the day of judgment and perdition of ungodly men (2 Peter 3:3–7).

"All Things Continue . . ."

Notice that the Scriptures are warning us that in the last days, people are going to be saying, "Everything goes on as it has since the beginning of creation." Secularists tell us that the earth has been in existence for millions of years and that life started evolving on this earth millions of years ago. Many Christians also hold this same belief. Geologists have the idea that the processes we see operating in the present world have been going on for millions of years at essentially the same rate and will probably go on for millions of years into the future as well. The technical word used in geology for this belief is *uniformitarianism*.[1] For example, the desert museum in Tucson, Arizona, not only has a display for people to see what supposedly has happened over the past millions of years, but it also has a display of what many scientists believe will happen in Arizona over the millions of years they believe are to come!

Evolutionists and those who believe in an old earth often use the phrase, "The present is the key to the past." In other words, they say the way to understand the past is to observe what happens in the present. For instance, they say that since fossils form rarely in today's world, the vast layers of rock containing billions of fossils over most of the earth's surface must have taken millions of years to form. Evolutionists tell us that since we observe mutations (that is, accidental changes in our genes) occurring today, these must have occurred ever since the dawn of time. Thus, mutations must be one of the mechanisms involved in the postulated evolutionary progression.

The Bible, on the other hand, tells us that there was a time when there was no sin, and thus there was neither animal nor human death, nor disease, nor mistakes. Mutations are *mistakes* that occur in our genes, and they are virtually all harmful. Those who believe in evolution have to assume that evolution is occurring today to be able to say that what we see today are the same processes that have gone on for millions of years. Thus, to be consistent, the Christian who believes in evolution should also believe that man is still evolving today.

How can we establish beyond doubt the details of an event that supposedly happened in the past? One way is to find witnesses who

---

1. For more information on uniformitarianism, see John Whitmore, "Aren't Millions of Years Required for Geological Processes?" in *The New Answers Book 2*, Ken Ham, editor (Green Forest, AR: Master Books, 2008), pp. 229–244; available online at http://www.answersingenesis.org/articles/nab2/arent-millions-of-years-required.

were there or look for records written by witnesses. Therefore, the only way we can ever know for sure exactly what happened in the geological past is if there was someone who was there at the time (a witness) who could tell us whether geological processes have always been the same or whether at some time geological processes have been different.

The Bible claims to be the record of One (God) who not only knows everything but who has always been there because He is outside of time. In fact, He created time. The Bible claims that God moved men through His Spirit to write down His words and that they are not just the words of men but the Word of God (1 Thess. 2:13; 2 Peter 1:20–21). The Book of Genesis claims to be the record from God telling us of the events of creation and of other events in this world's early history that have great bearing upon our present circumstances. Thus, the present is not the key to the past. Rather, revelation is the key to the past — and knowing what happened in the past is the key to understanding the present.

The revelation in Genesis tells us about such events as creation, the entrance of sin and death because of the Fall of man, Noah's Flood, and the Tower of Babel. These are events that have made the earth's geology, geography, biology, and so on what they are today. Therefore, we must also realize that what happened in the past is the key to the present. The entrance of sin into the world explains why we have death and why we have mistakes occurring in our genes. The global devastation caused by Noah's Flood helps to explain most of the fossil record. The events at the Tower of Babel help us to come to an understanding of the origin of the different nations and cultures around the world.

Today secularists deny that the biblical record in Genesis can be taken seriously. They are really putting their faith in their belief that "all things continue as they have done from the beginning." The prophecy in 2 Peter 3 is being fulfilled before our very eyes.

"Willingly Ignorant . . ."

In the next section of this prophecy we are told that men will deliberately reject three things. Notice that the emphasis here is on a deliberate rejection, or as some translations put it, a "willing igno-rance." Thus, it is a deliberate action on a person's part not to believe:

(a) God created the world, which at first was covered with water (which means that its surface was cool at the beginning, not a molten blob, as evolutionists teach);

(b) God once judged this world with a global, cataclysmic Flood at the time of Noah;

(c) God is going to judge this world again, but next time it will be by fire.

People often make the statement, "If there is so much evidence that God created the world and sent a global cataclysmic flood, then surely all scientists would believe this." The solution is given here in 2 Peter 3. It is not simply a matter of providing evidence to convince people, for people do not want to be convinced. We read in Romans 1:20 that there is enough evidence to convince everyone that God is Creator, so much so that we are condemned if we do not believe. Furthermore, Romans 1:18 tells us that men "suppress the truth in unrighteousness."

It is not a matter of lack of evidence to convince people that the Bible is true; the problem is that they do not *want* to believe the Bible. The reason for this is obvious. If people believed in the God of the Bible, they would have to acknowledge His authority and obey the rules He has laid down. However, every human being suffers from the same problem — the sin that Adam committed in the Garden of Eden, a disease that we all inherit. Adam's sin was rebellion against God's authority. Likewise, people everywhere today are in rebellion against God, so to admit that the Bible is true would be an admission of their own sinful and rebellious nature and of their need to be born again by cleansing through the blood of Christ.

It is easy to see this willing ignorance in action when watching debates over the origins issue. In most cases, the evolutionists are not interested in the wealth of data, evidence, and information the creationists put forward. They usually try to attack creationists by attempting to destroy their credibility. They are not interested in data, logical reasoning, or any evidence that points to creation or refutes evolution because they are totally committed to their religious faith called evolution.

One only has to go to the many secular sites on the Internet to read such attacks such as this one:

The king of the Answers in Genesis hucksters, Ken Ham, is panhandling for the fundamentalist institute in Modesto where they are holding a Creationist Conference. Ken's a big promoter of pseudo science methodology to try to "prove" that the earth is less than 10,000 years old. Sending children to be misinformed by this fundamentalist is borderline child abuse.[2]

Instead of looking at the data or reasoning behind biblical creationism, this blogger resorted to simply attacking the biblical creation ministry as "pseudo science" and "child abuse." Actually, such attacks only serve to confirm Romans 1 that such people "suppress the truth in unrighteousness" (Rom. 1:18).

Modern geology tells us that there never was a global Flood as described in the Bible. We are told that millions of years of geological processes can explain the enormous fossil record in the sedimentary rock layers over the earth's surface. However, creationists have shown that the fossil-bearing rock layers were produced by enormous catastrophic processes consistent with Noah's Flood.[3] But evolutionists refuse to accept this, for to do so would mean that the Bible is right, and thus the whole of their evolutionary philosophy would have to be rejected. These people are willingly ignorant about the facts that do not support their evolutionary ideas but do fit into a model of geology based upon what the Bible says concerning Noah's Flood. This is another fulfillment of prophecy before our very eyes.

Much of the scientific literature also tells us that most scientists expect this world to go on and on for millions of years. The example of the desert museum in Tucson, Arizona, is again appropriate. As mentioned before, one display at this museum is supposed to represent what scientists believe will happen in Arizona over the next few millions of years or so. People often look at that display and ask the

2. Randall Gross, "Ken Ham, Fundamentalist Huckster Panhandling in Modesto," Little Green Footballs (blog), http://littlegreenfootballs.com/page/261504.
3. In recent years, partly because of the success of creationist geologists in pointing out the clear evidence of rapid processes in rocks, many evolutionary geologists have begun to abandon the slow and gradual view in favor of the idea that there were many great catastrophes in the earth's history that were responsible for shaping it. However, their opposition to the catastrophe described in the Bible is as vehement and as willfully ignorant as ever.

question, "How can they know what is going to happen millions of years into the future?" The answer is, "In exactly the same way they understand what has happened millions of years in the past!" They do not know; it is only their guess.

If scientists agreed that God had created as outlined in Genesis, that Noah's Flood was a real event, and that, therefore, the Bible was true, they would have to tell quite a different account. The passage in 2 Peter makes it clear that God judged with water in the past (Noah's Flood), but that next time He will use fire as the method of judgment. Sinful man in rebellion against God does not want to admit that he must stand before the God of creation one day and account for his life. Thus, in rejecting creation and Noah's Flood, and claiming scientific evidence that supposedly supports his own belief, he becomes comfortable in not thinking about the coming judgment. But just as God created the world by His Word and sent the Flood through His Word, so God will judge this world by fire.

Conclusion

The earth, sun, moon, and stars stand as memorials to the fact that God has created. The fossil record is an immense memorial to

the fact that God has judged by water. All of this should warn each man, woman, and child that, just as God has kept His word in the past concerning judgment, so He will keep His word in the future concerning judgment.

Second Peter 3 contains a prophecy concerning the last days — a prophecy we are seeing fulfilled before our very eyes. Let us, therefore, become more vigorous and bold in witnessing for our God, the God of creation. "Therefore, since all these things will be dissolved, what manner of persons ought you to be in holy conduct and godliness, looking for and hastening the coming of the day of God" (2 Peter 3:11–12).

The late Isaac Asimov, an active anti-creationist, gave warnings about creationists. He was quoted as saying (in regard to creationists being given equal time for presenting the creation model in school), it is "today equal time, tomorrow the world." Isaac Asimov was right! We are out to convince the world that Jesus Christ is Creator. Isaac Asimov was one who signed the *Humanist Manifesto*; he was out to convince the world that Jesus Christ is not the Creator.

We are out to convince people like Isaac Asimov that Jesus Christ is Creator and Savior. Why? Because we want a good fight? Because we like controversy? No, because we know that those who do not trust the Lord will spend eternity separated from Him. And what happens to those of us who do receive the free gift of salvation offered by Christ?

> Behold, the tabernacle of God is with men, and He will dwell with them, and they shall be His people. God Himself will be with them and be their God. And God will wipe away every tear from their eyes; there shall be no more death, nor sorrow, nor crying. There shall be no more pain, for the former things have passed away (Rev. 21:3–4).

AN UNCERTAIN
SOUND

> And they were astonished at His teaching, for He taught
> them as one having authority, and not as the scribes (Mark
> 1:22).

A COUPLE OF YEARS AGO in Australia, a Christian member of
parliament appeared on national TV. He was on a panel that included
famed atheist Richard Dawkins of England. The moderator asked the
Christian, "So where did human beings come from?" The Christian
gently put his hand on Richard Dawkins's arm and replied, "Well,
you may well ask this guy. He's got firm views on that perspective
from there."[1]

Essentially, this well-known Australian Christian declared that
secularists know what they believe, but Christians do not. Sadly, the
way in which this Christian answered a legitimate question represents
the origins view of most Christians today.

---

1. Steve Fielding and Richard Dawkins, interview by Tony Jones, *Q&A: Adventures in Democracy*, ABC1 (Australia), March 8, 2010, http://www.abc.net.au/tv/qanda/txt/s2831712.htm.

There is an uncertain sound being blared by many in the Church. How can we be discerning? Think about it! When most Christians — including Christian academics, pastors, and other Christian leaders — are asked what they believe about Genesis, the answers can be one or more of the following:

- "There is a gap of millions of years between the first verses of Genesis."

- "We don't know what the days of Genesis mean."

- "The Flood was a local event. Fossils are probably millions of years old."

- "God used evolution to evolve Adam and Eve."

- "The framework idea fits millions of years into Genesis."

- "Genesis 1 is a poem."

- "Adam and Eve don't have to be literal people."

- "God made races of people to start with."

- "Genesis 1 represents the cosmic temple, not material origins."

I could go on and on. The point is, there are several compromise positions on Genesis that permeate the Church. All these views have one thing in common: they try to accommodate what the secularists believe about origins.

Think about this: most children from church homes attend public schools where, by and large, their textbooks and lectures (and even TV documentaries) give our young people a very specific history. Here is what they are almost always taught as fact:

The universe began with a big bang 15 billion years ago. The stars formed 10 billion years ago. The sun formed 5 billion years ago and the molten earth 4.5 billion years ago.

Water formed on the earth 3.8 billion years ago. And over millions of years, life formed from nonlife and then evolved to fish, then amphibians, reptiles, to birds and mammals, then apelike creatures, and then man — a process involving death over millions of years.

Secularists insist they know all of this happened in the unobservable past. They claim to know the true history of the universe. They believe and preach their worldview with zeal.

On the other hand, Christians have the benefit of a very specific history that has been revealed to them by Someone who was there at the beginning and throughout history — and who does not lie. Yet most believers say they are not sure what God said in Genesis!

No wonder we are seeing a mass exodus of young people from our churches! They begin to doubt the Bible in Genesis, reject it as God's Word, and then leave the Church. The Bible declares, "For if the trumpet makes an uncertain sound, who will prepare for battle?" (1 Cor. 14:8).

There is an uncertain sound being blared by much of the Church, including in Christian academia. Young people and adults in our churches are hearing (and often heeding) this uncertain sound about the accuracy of the Bible from its very start. As a result, many Christians are not really sure about what they believe. Meanwhile, they hear the secular world — speaking with authority — telling them they know exactly what to believe!

In Mark 1:22 we read that many people were astonished with Christ's teaching, for He spoke as one having authority. Today, we can speak with this same authority, because we have the Word of God! Jesus Christ, the Creator and the Word, has given us the Bible, and He told us how He created all things.

Furthermore, He has given us a very specific history from the Old Testament to the New Testament — a history that is foundational to all doctrine, including the gospel (in Genesis 3). It is the true history of the world that tells us where we all came from, what our problem is (sin), and what the solution is — salvation through Christ.

What a difference it would make if Christians started speaking with authority and then witnessed to the world! We do know what we believe — and it is the truth because it is the Word of God!

This is my challenge — let's get out there and give that certain sound! If all Christians did that, we could change the world!

MATURING THE MESSAGE: CREATIONISM AND BIBLICAL AUTHORITY IN THE CHURCH[1]

THE CREATION MESSAGE HAS MATURED over the past three decades as the discernment and understanding of creationist leaders has matured. More and more, the emphasis is on the foundational issue: compromise of Genesis ultimately undermines the gospel itself.

Many people are familiar with the diagrams that have become known as the "castle illustrations," which summarize the message of Answers in Genesis. These diagrams were first produced around 30 years ago as I endeavored to illustrate the concept of the foundational nature of the battle between Christianity and secular humanism.

However, the castle diagrams we use today have changed significantly over the years — even though the basic message has remained the same. One of those changes really reflects the maturation of the

---

1. This article is reprinted from *Answers* magazine, January–March 2010, p. 61–63.

biblical creation message as the Answers in Genesis ministry has been repositioned from being just a creation/evolution ministry to one of biblical authority.

You can see this shift in graphic form (see the following). In 1986, I was filmed at a church near Phoenix, Arizona, presenting a message on "The Relevance of Creation" (converted into a movie entitled *The Genesis Solution*). During that presentation, I used the castle diagrams that have become an icon of the Answers in Genesis ministry. The early castle diagram below shows two castles attacking each other with these words at the bottom of each castle: "Evolution" and "Creation."

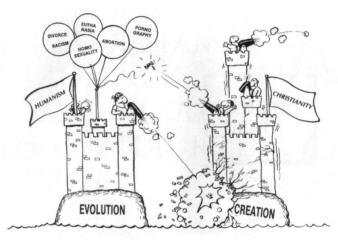

1986: An Early Castle Illustration

If you look at the bottom of the castle diagram I use today, you will read "Autonomous Human Reasoning" and "Revelation — God's Word." So why the change? I believe biblical creation ministry has made a vital shift in its thrust, which reflects a greater understanding of the real issue confronting our world. Biblical creation ministry now communicates in a way that reflects the true nature of the underlying battle concerning creation, evolution, and millions of years.

"Man Decides Truth" or "God's Word Is Truth"

Before I explain the recent change in detail, consider another version of the castle diagrams we have been using up until relatively

1987–2008: Modified Castle Illustration

recently. Note the words at the bottom of the castles: "Evolution — Man Decides Truth" and "Creation — God's Word Is Truth."

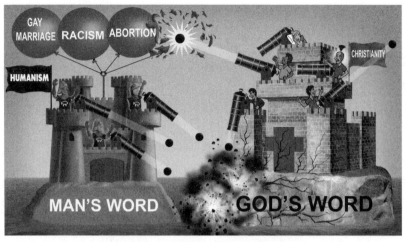

Current Castle Illustration

This diagram reflects the introduction of the change that has led to the emphasis that we bring today through these illustrations.

When I began teaching in public school in Australia in 1975, during one of my first science lessons, I vividly remember a student asking, "Mr. Ham, how can you be a Christian and believe in the Bible when we know it is not true?" I then asked the student why he would say that, and he replied, "Well, the Bible talks about Adam and Eve, but we know that is not true because our textbooks show us that we evolved from apes."

Right then I realized that the teaching of evolution was a big stumbling block preventing those students from being receptive to the gospel of Jesus Christ, so I began to develop ways of teaching about the creation/evolution issue. Around the same time, I was invited to speak in some local churches and Bible studies. I was shocked to find that most people (including most pastors and church leaders) either believed in evolution and/or millions of years, or they did not think it mattered what a person believed about the Book of Genesis.

As I developed my presentations and the illustrations that went with them, I often used the castle diagrams with creation and evolution as the foundation blocks. However, over time, I recognized that many people really did not understand something that I thought these foundational blocks clearly implied — that by "creation" I meant the revelation of God's Word and in particular the account of origins given in Scripture, and by "evolution" I meant that man determines truth, including the belief of origins developed by human reasoning.

Over time, I began to emphasize that believing in the creation account in Genesis means accepting God's Word as the ultimate authority, and believing in the secular idea of evolution is to accept man's word as the ultimate authority.

The Real Issues

As we mature as Christians, our spiritual discernment and understanding also mature. I am sure that is just one of the reasons why, even though I prayed for God to raise up the Creation Museum 30 years ago, He delayed the answer. The Lord knew we needed a lot of maturing in the message before He could open this great teaching center near Cincinnati that is reaching people around the world. When I make presentations now, not only do I talk about the problems with evolution/millions of years and how this undermines the authority of the Word of God, but I also teach two other things:

Genesis is the basis of all doctrine, including the gospel. First, I teach about the foundational importance of the book of Genesis — that the history in Genesis 1–11 is foundational to all Christian doctrine, including the gospel itself. I do this to remind Christians that they cannot defend any doctrines unless they first believe that Genesis 1–11 is literal history (as Jesus did, for instance, in defending marriage by quoting Genesis in Matthew 19:4–7).

Reinterpreting Genesis undermines the Word of God itself. However, there is another vital aspect that needs to be understood. This is vital for Christians to understand, and the biblical creation movement needs to be shouting this message from the rooftops. That is, when Christians reinterpret the days of creation to fit with millions of years, reinterpret Genesis 1:1 to fit with the big bang, or adopt other positions that add Darwinian evolution to the Bible, they are undermining the very Word of God itself. And this is the issue; this is why we have lost biblical authority from the culture.

As I remind Christians, we know that Jesus rose from the dead because we take God's Word as it is written. Secular scientists have never shown that a dead body can be raised to life, but we do not reinterpret the Resurrection as a nonliteral event. We take God's Word as written. Yet in Genesis, so many Christians (including most Christian leaders) accept secular scientists' old-earth ideas and reinterpret the creation account. In doing so they have unlocked a door — the door to undermining biblical authority. Subsequent generations usually push that door open further. This is what has happened across Europe and the United Kingdom, and it is happening across America.

For those involved in ministry of any kind, I challenge you to recognize a crucial, modern application of Psalm 11:3, "If the foundations are destroyed, what can the righteous do?" Applied to where we are today, the foundational issues are not ultimately creation and evolution but God's Word versus autonomous human reasoning. This is the same battle that began in Genesis 3:1 when the serpent said to the woman, "Has God indeed said . . . ?"

That sums up what the creation/evolution battle is all about. It's all about authority — God's infallible Word or autonomous man's fallible word!

MILLIONS OF YEARS OR EVOLUTION: WHICH IS THE GREATER THREAT?[1]

WHEN THE SECULAR MEDIA visit the Creation Museum to interview me, they rarely ask about biological evolution. Typically they will start by asking, "Why do you believe dinosaurs and people lived at the same time?" or "What do you believe about the age of the earth?" or even, "Why do you reject science and believe God created the universe in six days only thousands of years ago?"

I believe they start this way because they know biological evolution is impossible without billions of years of history. In fact, I find that secularists are very emotionally committed to the millions and billions of years. They almost go ballistic when told the earth is only thousands of years old.

In my experience, I have found that secularists do not really care if Christians reject evolution. Yes, they still mock. But the minute people reject billions of years, they are labeled anti-science, anti-academic, and

1. This article is reprinted from *Answers* magazine, July–September 2012, p. 26–29.

anti-intellectual. The pressure to believe in an old earth is extremely great.

Problem #1: Loss of Biblical Authority

Secularists understand something few Christians seem to grasp — that biological evolution is not the heart of the issue. The concept of millions of years is. If they accept a history time-line as outlined in the Bible (around 6,000 years), secularists are forced to abandon evolution, and creation is the only viable alternative. But by accepting an old earth, it is easy for them to justify their rejection of God and the trustworthiness of His Word.

Most conservative, evangelical pastors recognize that the Scriptures clearly teach Adam was made from dust and Eve was made from his side. They realize how hard it would be to explain the gospel without referring to the origin of sin and death in Genesis. However, many such pastors do not consider the age of the earth to be an important issue.

All of the compromised positions on Genesis (the gap theory, framework hypothesis, theistic evolution, day-age theory, progressive creation, and others) have one thing in common: they attempt to fit millions of years of history into Genesis 1. The major reason so many pastors, Christian academics, and Christians do not believe in six literal (24-hour) days of creation is ultimately their desire to account for the supposed billions of years.

Such compromise places mankind's fallible dating methods — his *beliefs* about the past — in authority over God's Word. This opens a door to undermining biblical authority. Such compromise does not negate one's salvation, but it does affect how coming generations view Scripture.

Problem #2: Loss of the Next Generation

This compromise causes a generational loss of biblical authority. Loss of authority is a major reason many young people doubt the Bible and ultimately walk away from the Church. This slide was documented in research published in the book *Already Gone*, which showed clearly why and when the Church is losing about two-thirds of the next generation.

The concept of millions of years flies directly in the face of the history God's Word clearly reveals. Ultimately, belief in millions of years attacks the character of God. If the fossil-bearing layers were laid down slowly over millions of years, then these layers contain the remains of dead creatures, fossil thorns, evidence of diseases (e.g., brain tumors), and animals eating each other — all before humans appeared on the planet.

How can a Christian fit this into God's Word, which tells us that everything was "very good" after God finished creating man? How can a good God call brain tumors "very good"? How could such history fit with Scripture, which tells us that thorns came after sin and that humans and animals were originally all vegetarian?

Problem #3: Origin in Philosophical Naturalism

The old age of the earth is a much bigger problem than biological evolution. Not only is it a direct attack on the authority of Scripture that drives away the next generation, but it is also the child of the pagan religion of this age — naturalism, the atheistic philosophy that everything can be explained by natural causes without God. Secularists must cling to long ages to explain life without a Creator.

Belief in an old earth was born out of naturalism, as documented by the research of Terry Mortenson.[2] The belief in billions of years was originally postulated by materialists, atheists, and deists in an attempt to explain the geological record by natural processes rather than by a global Flood, as revealed in the Bible.

Naturalism is the anti-God religion of this age, and the concept of millions of years is foundational to its false idea of biological evolution. George Wald, a biochemist and Nobel Prize winner, explains why a long period of time is so important to evolution's story: "Time is in fact the hero of the plot. The time . . . is of the order of two billion years. What we regard as impossible on the basis of human experience is meaningless here. Given so much time, the 'impossible' becomes possible, the possible probable, and the probable virtually certain. One has only to wait: time itself performs the miracles."[3]

---

2. "Philosophical Naturalism and the Age of the Earth: Are They Related?" *The Master's Seminary Journal* 15 (1): p. 71–92.
3. "The Origin of Life," *Scientific American* 191: p. 48.

Without the belief in millions of years, Charles Darwin could never have successfully postulated his ideas of biological evolution. One figure who probably did more than anyone else to popularize belief in millions of years is Charles Lyell, who published his ideas in *The Principles of Geology* (1830). Darwin took Lyell's work with him in his five-year voyage aboard the ship HMS *Beagle*. Lyell's book convinced Darwin and gave him the foundation to propose millions of years of small changes in biology.[4]

On the surface, it does seem really radical to reject millions of years. If you visit museums, zoos, and even amusement parks like Disneyland, EPCOT, and Universal Studios, you will hear and see the phrase "millions of years" much more than the word *evolution*. You have to watch only one or two documentaries on Discovery Channel, the Learning Channel, or the History Channel to hear the words "millions [or billions] of years" multiple times. Even the leading children's museum in the USA, the Indianapolis Children's Museum, has numerous signs in its dinosaur exhibit with the words "millions of years." But one will be hard-pressed to find the word *evolution*.

Standing against biological evolution only partly closes the door to biblical compromise. Refusing to compromise on the time-line of God's Word beginning in Genesis — while standing against mankind's fallible beliefs about millions of years — slams the door completely shut.

As an analogy, the idea of millions of years is like a disease (although we know sin is everyone's ultimate disease). Biological evolution is merely the symptom. Many Christians are treating the symptom but fail to recognize the source disease.

Time may be the hero of the secular evolutionary plot, but the hero of real events is God. In Scripture He has given us the infallible record of the true history of the universe, which shows how He has been working out His plan to redeem sinners since Adam brought death into the world around 6,000 years ago.

---

4. Ibid.

OTHER "INTERPRETATIONS" OF GENESIS[1]

THE PURPOSE OF THIS SECTION is to define some of the interpretive schemes that have arisen since the idea of vast ages became popular in the late 18th and early 19th centuries. Please bear in mind that old-earth theologies were essentially nonexistent prior to 1800. This fact alone provides strong evidence that these views are not derived from the Bible. Instead, they are an attempt to accommodate the long ages promoted by uniformitarian science.

The Gap Theory

This was the first attempt to harmonize the biblical account of creation with the idea of vast ages. It claims that a huge time gap (perhaps several billion years) exists between Genesis 1:1 and Genesis 1:2. In the most popular ruin-and-reconstruction version, it is said that during this time, Satan rebelled and led creation in rebellion against God. As a result, God destroyed this original creation with

---

1. Portions of this appendix were taken from Tim Chaffey and Jason Lisle, *Old-Earth Creationism on Trial* (Green Forest, AR: Master Books, 2008).

the flood of Lucifer. Gap theorists believe that Genesis 1:2 describes the conditions of the world following this flood.

A young Presbyterian minister, Thomas Chalmers, began to preach this idea in 1804. In 1814, he published this idea and the gap theory began to enjoy a great deal of acceptance in the Church. Gap theorists often argue that the word translated as "was" in most English versions of Genesis 1:2 should actually be translated "became" as in "the earth became formless and void." However, this is unwarranted by context. The gap theory suffers from a number of hermeneutical problems.

First, time cannot be inserted between Genesis 1:1 and Genesis 1:2 because verse 2 does not follow verse 1 in time. Verse 2 uses a Hebrew grammatical device called a "waw-disjunctive." This is where a sentence begins with the Hebrew word for "and" ("waw" ו) followed by a noun such as the "earth" ("erets" ארץ). A waw-disjunctive indicates that the sentence is describing the previous one; it does not follow in time. In other words, verse 2 is describing the conditions of the earth when it was first created. Hebrew grammar does not allow for the insertion of vast periods of time between Genesis 1:1 and 1:2.

Second, Exodus 20:11 clearly teaches that everything was created in the span of six days; this is the basis for our workweek. This passage clearly precludes any possibility of vast periods of time between any of the days of creation.

Third, most versions of the gap theory put death and suffering long before Adam's sin, so the gap theory suffers from many of the same doctrinal problems as the day-age view. For a full refutation of the gap theory, please read Unformed and Unfilled by Weston W. Fields.[2]

Theistic Evolution

This view claims that God used evolution as a means of bringing about His creation. Conservative Christians typically reject this idea because it attacks the idea that Adam was made in the image of God and from the dust of the earth. Instead, he and Eve simply

---

2. Weston Fields, *Unformed and Unfilled* (Green Forest, AR: Master Books, 2005).

evolved from apelike creatures. Many liberal scholars accept this view and see no problem with incorporating evolutionary principles into the Bible.

Theistic evolution impugns the character of God by blaming Him for millions of years of death, bloodshed, disease, and suffering. A world with these things in it could hardly be called "very good." As with day-age and gap theories, theistic evolution is not supported by Scripture and has numerous doctrinal problems.

The Day-Age Theory

This view is appropriately named. Its proponents claim that each of the days of creation was an extremely long period of time. In support of this view, they usually quote Psalm 90:4 and 2 Peter 3:8, which state "one day is as a thousand years."

The problem with citing these verses is that they are not even referring to creation. The passage in 2 Peter, for example, is referring to the Second Coming. These verses are simply teaching that God is not limited by time. He is beyond the confines of His creation, not bound by it.

The day-age theory became popular after George Stanley Faber, a respected Anglican bishop, began to teach it in 1823. For the past two centuries, this view has been tweaked to accommodate changing scientific beliefs. Some day-age proponents believe in theistic evolution; others believe in progressive creation, as described below. The day-age view is based on a hermeneutical error called an "unwarranted expansion of an expanded semantic field." In other words, it is assumed that because the Hebrew word for "day" can mean "time" (in a general sense) in some contexts, then it is permissible to interpret it to mean "time" in Genesis 1. However, the context of Genesis 1 does not allow for such a possibility.

Progressive Creation

This version of old-earth creationism is probably the most popular of the compromise views in the Church today. Most progressive creationists are also day-age supporters; they believe that each of the creation days was a long period of time. However, rather than accepting biological evolution, progressive creationists believe that

God created in stages over many millions of years. They believe that God created certain animals millions of years ago and then they died out. Then God created more animals that died out. Eventually, He got around to making humans.

Although many progressive creationists reject biological evolution, they generally accept astronomical and geological evolution. Like theistic evolutionists, progressive creationists believe in millions of years of death, disease, suffering, and bloodshed before Adam's sin. Such positions inevitably undermine the Gospel message.

Dr. Hugh Ross's organization, Reasons to Believe, is the leading promoter of this view today.

Framework Hypothesis[3]

In 1924 Arie Noordtzij developed the framework hypothesis. Approximately 30 years later, Meredith Kline popularized the view in the United States, while N.H. Ridderbos did the same in Europe. It is currently one of the most popular views of Genesis 1 being taught in seminaries. Despite its popularity in academia, laypeople in our churches have not heard this view fully explained, though they have heard of some of its claims.

The framework hypothesis is essentially an attempt to reclassify the genre of Genesis 1 as being something other than historical narrative. Proponents have attempted to identify figurative language or semi-poetic devices in the text. Thinking they have successfully shown that the Bible's first chapter is not to be taken in its plain sense, they make the claim that Genesis 1 simply reveals that God created everything and that He made man in His own image, but it gives us no information about how or when He did this.

A premise that all framework advocates agree with is the two triads of "days" argument. Framework supporters claim that the two triads of "days" is a topical parallelism where the topics of days 1 through 3 are parallel with those of days 4 through 6. About the parallel nature of days 1 and 4, Mark Futato states, "Days 1 and 4

---

3. The information on the framework hypothesis was taken from Tim Chaffey and Bob McCabe's article, "Framework Hypothesis," in *How Do We Know the Bible Is True?* Vol. 1, Ken Ham and Bodie Hodge, editors (Green Forest, AR: Master Books, 2011), p. 189–199.

are two different perspectives on the same creative work."[4] In other words, days 1 and 4 are simply two different ways of stating the same event, as are days 2 and 5, and days 3 and 6. The following chart is representative of that used by many framework advocates and reflects this topical parallelism.[5]

Day	Formation of the World (Items Created)	Day	Filling of the World (Items Created)
1	darkness, light	4	heavenly light-bearers
2	heavens, water	5	birds of the air, water animals
3	seas, land, vegetation	6	land animals, man, provision of food

At first glance, it may seem as if these writers are on to something. However, a closer look reveals some problems with this argument. First, this supposed semi-poetic construction is inconsistent with the fact that Genesis 1 is a historical narrative. Hebrew scholar Stephen Boyd has clearly shown that Genesis 1 is written as historical narrative rather than poetry.

Second, the above chart is inconsistent with the text of Genesis 1:1–2:3. Water was not created on the second day but the first (Gen. 1:2). Another problem with this chart is that the "heavenly light-bearers" of day 4 were placed in the "heavens" of day 2 (Gen. 1:14). This is problematic for the framework advocate who believes days 1 and 4 are the same event viewed from different perspectives, because this must have occurred prior to the event described in days 2 and 5. How could the stars be placed in something that did not exist yet?

Finally, the order of events is crucial here. The framework proposes that the days are not chronological but theological. However, if one rearranges the chronology, then it breaks down into absurdity.

---

4. Mark D. Futato, "Because It Had Rained: A Study of Gen 2:5–7 with Implications for Gen 2:4–25 and Gen 1:1–2:3," *Westminster Theological Journal* 60 (Spring 1998): p. 16.

5. William VanGemeren, *The Progress of Redemption: The Story of Salvation from Creation to the New Jerusalem* (Grand Rapids, MI: Baker, 1988), p. 47.

Temple Inauguration View

Also called the cosmic temple position, this idea was popularized by John Walton, professor of Old Testament at Wheaton College. Walton draws on ancient Near Eastern mythologies because he believes they help today's readers understand how the original readers of Genesis thought. His point in doing this, however, is to make the case for why Genesis 1–2 cannot be read as history:

> The problem is, we cannot translate their cosmology to our cosmology, nor should we. If we accept Genesis 1 as ancient cosmology, then we need to interpret it as ancient cosmology rather than translate it into modern cosmology. If we try to turn it into modern cosmology, we are making the text say something it never said.[6]

Walton claims that the creation account in Genesis does not teach a physical creation, but rather a "nonfunctional" earth being made "functional." Similar to the framework hypothesis, Walton splits the six days of creation into two parts: the first three days for God to make the heavens and earth functional, and the second three days for God to create "functionaries," such as the sun, moon, and stars.

God's purpose in making the cosmos functional, according to the temple inauguration view, is that He was building Himself a temple. Walton explains that the seven days of Genesis 1 are not days of creation but days of inauguration:

> In summary, we have suggested that the seven days are not given as the period of time over which the material cosmos came into existence, but the period of time devoted to the inauguration of the functions of the cosmic temple, and perhaps also its annual reenactment. . . . Genesis 1 focuses on the creation of the (cosmic) temple, not the material phase of preparation.[7]

John Walton's argument in favor of this view of Genesis is driven by a desire to harmonize what modern science says about origins (i.e.,

---

6. John H. Walton, *The Lost World of Genesis One: Ancient Cosmology and the Origins Debate* (Downers Grove, IL: InterVarsity Press, 2009), p. 17.
7. Ibid., p. 92.

evolution/millions of years) with what Genesis teaches. If Genesis 1–2 is not a literal account of creation but instead a time of God making His "cosmic temple" functional, then millions of years/evolutionary ideas can be mixed with Genesis. And indeed, Walton writes, "If Genesis 1 does not require a young earth and if divine fiat does not preclude a long process, then Genesis 1 offers no objections to biological evolution. Biological evolution is capable of giving us insight into God's creative work."[8]

The temple inauguration view leaves the historical aspects of the creation account in Genesis behind in favor of an interpretation that allows evolution/millions of years to be mixed with Scripture. The view does not allow God, the One who was there at the beginning, to be the Creator; instead, it relegates Him to the role of making an already existent cosmos functional.

Historic Creation

The historic creation view, which is really a modified gap theory, was popularized by John Sailhamer. Many proponents of the historic creation view believe that God created the heavens and the earth over an indefinite period of time in Genesis 1:1. Then in Genesis 1:2 and following, proponents claim, God prepared the uninhabitable land for man in six days.

Mark Driscoll, pastor of Mars Hill Church in Seattle, Washington, holds the historic creation view and describes it in an article:

> In this view, Genesis 1:1 records the making of all of creation by God out of nothing (or ex nihilo) through a merism of "heavens and earth," which means the sky above and land below, or the totality of creation. Since the word used for "beginning" in Genesis 1:1 is *reshit* in Hebrew, which means an indefinite period of time, it is likely that all of creation was completed over an extended period of time (anywhere from days to billions of years). Then Genesis 1:2 begins the description of God preparing the uninhabitable land for the creation of mankind. The preparation of the uncultivated land for and creation of Adam and Eve occurred in six literal

---

8. Ibid., p. 138.

twenty-four hour days. This view leaves open the possibility of both an old earth and six literal days of creation.[9]

The historic creation view, as Driscoll clearly says, is simply an attempt to harmonize millions of years with the literal account of creation in Genesis. Furthermore, the word *reshit* does not mean "an indefinite period of time," as Driscoll claims. It means "beginning, chief," or "first."[10] By itself, the word does not explain how long ago the beginning was, but that information is provided in Scripture. The beginning started the first day, and God created everything in six days and rested for one. Based on the genealogies given in Scripture, we can determine that this took place about 6,000 years ago.

Other Views

There have been other attempts to synchronize the Bible's account of creation with the evolutionary viewpoint. Two of these views have diminished in popularity in the past few decades. The *revelatory day* view states that God gave Moses a series of visions of His creative work. These visions lasted for six days. The obvious problem with this view is that there is absolutely no scriptural support for it. The Bible never even hints that this may have been the case, so it is based on a lack of evidence.

The other view is called the *literal-day-with-gaps*. This view states that each of the days of creation was a literal day, but there were huge gaps of time in between each day. This view suffers from many of the same problems as the day-age theory and the gap theory.

Numerous other minor views have been proposed in an effort to harmonize Genesis 1–11 with secular scientific opinion. Those described here represent the vast majority of believers who seek this harmonization. The very fact that so many views exist provides evidence that each of them is inherently flawed.

---

9. Mark Driscoll, "Answers to Common Questions about Creation," The Resurgence, http://theresurgence.com/2006/07/03/answers-to-common-questions-about-creation.

10. Francis Brown, Samuel Rolles Driver, and Charles Augustus Briggs, *Enhanced Brown-Driver-Briggs Hebrew and English Lexicon*, electronic ed. (Oak Harbor, WA: Logos Research Systems, 2000), 912.1.

RESOURCES

The following list of resources is recommended for researching further into the topics referred to in this book.

All books can be obtained in the United States through Master Books and Answers in Genesis. Addresses are given in section 18 below.

1. *A Is for Adam: The Gospel from Genesis* — Ken and Mally Ham (Green Forest, AR: Master Books, 2011). This is a children's rhyme book with notes designed to give you background information for each rhyme, thus equipping you to explain the concepts in greater detail. It is like reading a commentary on the Book of Genesis!

2. *Already Compromised* — Ken Ham and Greg Hall, with Britt Beemer (Green Forest, AR: Master Books, 2011). AiG president Ken Ham and college president Dr. Greg Hall team up for this eye-opening assessment of what administrators and professors of Christian colleges actually believe and teach regarding the Bible and science. The findings are shocking! Read this book to help you determine which Christian colleges will build — and which will damage — your child's faith.

3. *Already Gone* — Ken Ham and Britt Beemer, with Todd Hillard (Green Forest, AR: Master Books, 2009). In the first scientific study of its kind, the "Beemer Report" reveals startling facts discovered through 20,000 phone calls and detailed surveys of a thousand 20- to 29-year-olds who used to attend evangelical churches on a regular basis, but have since left it behind. In this powerful book, popular author Ken Ham and consumer behavior research/analyst Britt Beemer combine to reveal trends that must be dealt with now . . . before we lose another generation!

4. *Coming to Grips with Genesis* — Dr. Terry Mortenson and Dr. Thane Ury, editors (Green Forest, AR: Master

Books, 2008). Fourteen scholars present rigorous biblical and theological arguments in favor of a young earth and global Flood and also address a number of contemporary old-earth interpretations of Genesis. Featuring authors such as Dr. Henry Morris, Dr. John MacArthur, Dr. Steven Boyd, Dr. Terry Mortenson, Dr. Thane Ury, and more. (Semi-techinical)

5. *Creation: Facts of Life* — Dr. Gary Parker (Green Forest, AR: Master Books, 2006). A leading creation scientist and speaker presents the classic arguments for evolution used in public schools, universities, and the media, and refutes them in an entertaining and easy-to-read style. Once an evolutionist, Dr. Parker is well qualified to refute these arguments. A must-have for students and teachers alike.

6. *Earth's Catastrophic Past: Geology, Creation, and the Flood* — Dr. Andrew Snelling (Dallas, TX: Institute for Creation Research, 2009). This huge 2-volume set is filled with up-to-date geological evidence that demonstrates the authority and accuracy of the Bible's account of creation and the Flood. Geologist Dr. Andrew Snelling examines and deconstructs evolutionary interpretations of the geologic record and then constructs a biblical geological model for earth history and concludes that the claims of Genesis 1–11 are true. (Technical)

7. *Evolution Exposed: Biology and Earth Science* — Roger Patterson (Hebron, KY: Answers in Genesis, 2006, 2008). Tens of millions of teens have been taught the lie that evolution is a fact. It's not. In fact, the idea of evolution isn't even a good theory. Unfortunately, even the teachers of today's youth are unaware of the vast evidences against evolution, the evidences that support creation. Roger Patterson, an AiG writer and former public school teacher, exposes the evidences against evolution in these two excellent resources.

8. *The Great Turning Point* — Dr. Terry Mortenson (Green Forest, AR: Master Books, 2004). Many people in the Church today think that "young-earth" creationism is a fairly recent invention, popularized by fundamentalist Christians in the mid-20th century. Dr. Terry Mortenson presents his fascinating original research, which details the early-19th century origin of the idea of millions of years and the Christian men who opposed that idea.

9. *The New Answers Books 1, 2 and 3* — Ken Ham, general editor (Green Forest, AR: Master Books, 2006, 2008, 2010). Now you can have at your fingertips solid answers to the big questions about the Christian faith, evolution, creation, and the biblical worldview. Featuring authors such as Ken Ham, Dr. David Menton, Dr. Andrew Snelling, Dr. Georgia Purdom, Dr. Terry Mortenson, and others, each stand-alone chapter will give Christians answers to questions about topics like Noah's Flood, six-day creation, human and chimp DNA, cloning and stem cells, and many more. Also available on DVD in a mini-interview format with our authors.

10. *Old-Earth Creationism on Trial* — Tim Chaffey and Dr. Jason Lisle (Green Forest, AR: Master Books, 2008). Many churches have abandoned the Genesis account, that God created in six literal days. In a vital discussion focused within the Church, Tim Chaffey and Dr. Jason Lisle explore the foundational issues around the debate on the age of the earth, and they reveal the debate has a much more compelling and simple core truth — scriptural authority.

11. *One Race One Blood: A Biblical Answer to Racism* — Ken Ham and Dr. Charles Ware (Green Forest, AR: Master Books, 2010). It is a rarely discussed fact of history that the premise of Darwinian evolution has been deeply rooted in the worst racist ideology since its inception. The tragic legacy of Darwin's controversial speculations on evolution

has led to terrible consequences taken to the deadliest extremes. This book reveals the origins of these horrors, as well as the truth revealed in Scripture that God created only one race.

12. *Raising Godly Children in an Ungodly World* — Ken Ham and Steve Ham (Green Forest, AR: Master Books, 2008). As fathers and as sons of parents who instilled a legacy of faith within them, popular creation speaker Ken Ham and his brother Steve share from their hearts how they have used the Bible to guide them as they raise their children with the goal of instilling a legacy of faith within each. With Bible-based practical advice, this unique parenting book makes a great guide for parents with children of any age.

13. *Why Won't They Listen? The Power of Creation Evangelism* — Ken Ham (Green Forest, AR: Master Books, 2003). This revolutionary book by AiG president Ken Ham has already opened the eyes of thousands of Christians showing why the traditional methods of evangelism are not reaching today's humanistic, evolutionized culture. Endorsed by Dr. D. James Kennedy of Evangelism Explosion/Coral Ridge Presbyterian Church.

14. *The Young Earth, Revised and Expanded* — Dr. John D. Morris (Green Forest, AR: Master Books, 2007). Dr. John Morris, a geologist, explains in easy-to-understand terms how true science supports a young earth. Filled with facts that will equip laymen and scientists alike.

15. *Answers in Genesis newsletter*, published monthly by Answers in Genesis. To subscribe, visit www.AnswersInGenesis.org/go/newsletters.

16. *Answers* magazine, published quarterly by Answers in Genesis. For subscription information or to subscribe, visit www.AnswersInGenesis.org/go/am.

17. *Speakers Available for Conferences* — Speakers gifted and trained in presenting biblical and/or scientific aspects of the creation/evolution controversy — from layman through technical level — are available for teaching, preaching, debates, etc. For more information or to request an event, visit www.AnswersConferences.org.

18. *Other Books and Resources* — For a comprehensive listing of books and other resources available on the creation/evolution issue, contact the following organizations:

Master Books
P.O. Box 726
Green Forest, AR 72638
www.masterbooks.net

Answers in Genesis
P.O. Box 510
Hebron, KY 41048
www.AnswersinGenesis.org

Answers in Genesis
P.O. Box 8078
Leicester, LE21 9AJ
United Kingdom
www.AnswersinGenesis.org

ABOUT THE AUTHOR

KEN HAM IS THE PRESIDENT/CEO AND FOUNDER of Answers in Genesis–US and the highly acclaimed Creation Museum and is the visionary behind the construction of a full-size Noah's ark to be built south of Cincinnati. He has become one of the most in-demand Christian conference speakers and talk show guests in America.

A biblical apologist, Ken gives numerous faith-building talks to tens of thousands of children and adults each year on topics such as the reliability of the Bible, how compromise over biblical authority has undermined society and even the Church, witnessing more effectively, dinosaurs, "races," and more. Ken co-founded AiG in 1994 with the purpose of upholding the authority of the Bible from the very first verse.

Ken is the author of many books on Genesis, including *Already Gone*, co-authored by researcher Britt Beemer on why so many young people have left the Church, the best-selling *The Lie: Evolution*, and a number of children's books (*Dinosaurs for Kids, D Is for Dinosaur, A Is for Adam*, the new book *The True Account of Adam and Eve*, and others). Other recent co-authored books include *One Race, One Blood* and the provocative book *Already Compromised* about Christian colleges and how they treat the authority of the Bible.

Under his direction, AiG launched an impressive Sunday school curriculum in 2012 called *Answers Bible Curriculum*, which covers all 66 books of the Bible (seven age levels, from kindergarten through adult). Throughout, *ABC* defends the Bible's accuracy and authority, with the gospel presented.

Ken is heard daily on the radio feature *Answers . . . with Ken Ham* (broadcast on more than 500 stations) and is a frequent guest on national TV talk-show programs. Since the Creation Museum opened in 2007, he has been interviewed on *CBS News Sunday Morning, The NBC Nightly News* with Brian Williams, *The PBS News Hour* with Jim Lehrer, and many other outlets. The museum, located in northern Kentucky and near Cincinnati, has drawn over 1.6 million visitors in five years.

Ken is also the founder of the award-winning *Answers* magazine, which won the prestigious Award of Excellence (for top Christian magazine) in both 2011 and 2012 from the Evangelical Press Association. He also writes articles for AiG's popular website www.AnswersInGenesis.org, which was the 2012 recipient of the Best Ministry Website as awarded by the 1,200-member National Religious Broadcasters. The AiG website receives over a million web visitors a month.

Ken's bachelor's degree in applied science (with an emphasis on environmental biology) was awarded by the Queensland Institute of Technology in Australia. He also holds a diploma of education from the University of Queensland (a graduate qualification necessary for Ken to begin his initial career as a science teacher in the public schools in Australia).

In recognition of the contribution Ken has made to the Church in the United States and internationally, Ken has been awarded four honorary doctorates: a Doctor of Divinity (1997) from Temple Baptist College in Cincinnati, Ohio; a Doctor of Literature (2004) from Liberty University in Lynchburg, Virginia; a Doctor of Letters (2010) from Tennessee Temple University; and a Doctorate in Humane Letters from Mid-Continent University in Kentucky (2012).

Ken and his wife, Mally, reside in the Cincinnati area. They have five children and ten grandchildren.

Ken Ham Time-line

1974   Ken Ham obtains a copy of *The Genesis Flood* book.

1975   Ken Ham begins his teaching career at Dalby State High School in Queensland, Australia. His science students challenge him about believing the Bible because of the evolution teaching in the science textbooks.

1975   Ken Ham gives his first ever talk on creation apologetics at a Baptist church in Brisbane, Australia.

1977   Ken Ham and John Mackay hold first creation seminar. Ken, a science teacher, and his wife, Mally, and science teacher John Mackay begin two ministries out of Ken and Mally's home in Australia: a book outreach called Creation Science Supplies and a teaching ministry called Creation Science Educational Media Services.

1979   At a special service at their church, Sunnybank Baptist in Brisbane, Australia, the pastor and deacons lay hands on Ken and Mally to set them apart to the work of creation ministry.

1979 Ken leaves teaching for full-time creation ministry.

1980 On February 15, Creation Science Supplies and Creation Science Educational Media Services are merged and become the Creation Science Foundation.

1981 Ken goes on his first speaking tour in the United States.

1981-1985 Ken involved in full-time teaching ministry in Australia and speaking tours in the United States. During this time, CSF board member John Thallon and Ken Ham kneel before the Lord on a piece of property south of Brisbane and pray for a Creation Museum.

1986 Ken, Mally, and their four children move to Arizona for six months to work with Films for Christ; *The Genesis Solution* (film/video) is recorded at Grace Community Church in Tempe, Arizona, and is released in 1987.

1986 *Understanding Genesis* (a 10-part video series with Ham and Dr. Gary Parker) is filmed in New South Wales, Australia.

1987 Ken is loaned by CSF to Dr. Henry Morris's Institute for Creation Research (ICR) in California as a speaker. Dr. Henry Morris's son John Morris has since assumed the role of president. The Hams move to the United States on January 22.

Ken and John Morris of ICR in Alaska

1987 Release of the book *The Lie: Evolution* and the film/video *The Genesis Solution* by Films for Christ

1988 *The Genesis Solution* (book) and *Creation and the Last Days* (video) are released by CLP Video/Master Books.

1990 *The Answers Book; What Really Happened to the Dinosaurs?* (children's book); *The Genesis Foundation* (3-part video series) by CLP Video; *Back to Genesis* (11-part video series for ICR)

1991 *Genesis and the Decay of the Nations* (book); *D Is for Dinosaur* (children's book)

1992 *The Answers Book*, updated; *Creation and the Christian Faith* (video), *Answers in Genesis* (video); *D Is for Dinosaur* (video) for the Creation Science Foundation/Master Books

1993 Ken resigns from ICR late in the year with the vision of beginning his own layperson-oriented creation ministry; Dr. Morris becomes one of the first donors to the new ministry.

1994 Ken, along with Mark Looy and Mike Zovath, founds Creation Science Ministries (CSM), later to be Answers in Genesis.

Ken, Mark, and Mike —
the beginning of
Answers in Genesis

1994	In March/April, the Hams, Looys, and Zovaths move from southern California to northern Kentucky in new ministry headquarters; CSM's first "Answers in Genesis" conference is held in Denver, Colorado, in March, drawing 2,200 adults and over 4,000 students. The first ministry newsletter was mailed out in March as well.

1994   In October, the *Answers . . . with Ken Ham* radio program begins airing. The CSM board meets late in the year and decides to change the ministry's name to Answers in Genesis (AiG) to reflect the ministry's focus on the authority of the Bible as well as apologetics.

1994   *Genesis and the Decay of the Nations*, updated book; *Answers in Genesis* (12-part video series with Ken Ham and Dr. Gary Parker), Master Books

1995   AiG's first website is designed & launched.

1995   *A Is for Adam* children's book is released.

1996   *The Answers Book*, updated again; *The Lie: Evolution*, updated edition; AiG produces three videos: *The Family Answers Video: Raising Godly Children in an Ungodly World; Evolution: The Anti-God Religion of Death*; and *A Is for Adam: The Gospel from Genesis*

1997   *And God Saw That It Was Good* (book); *The Monkey Trial: The Scopes Trial and the Decline of the Church* (video by AiG); *Dinosaurs: Missionary Lizards to the Lost World* (video by AiG)

1998   Two books released: *Creation Evangelism for the New Millennium; The Great Dinosaur Mystery Solved!* (Master Books)

1999 *The Answers Book: Updated and Expanded*; co-authored book *One Blood: The Biblical Answer to Racism*, English and Spanish editions; *The Lie: Evolution*, updated edition; book *Did Adam Have a Belly Button?*; *One Blood: The Biblical Answer to Racism* (video by AiG); *Answers . . . with Ken Ham* (12-part video series, co-produced with Cedarville University)

2000 *The Answers Book: Revised and Expanded*, English and Spanish editions; *No Retreats, No Reserves, No Regrets: Why Christians Should Never Give Up, Never Hold Back, and Never Be Sorry for Proclaiming Their Faith*

2001 *Creation Evangelism for the New Millennium*, Spanish edition; *The Lie: Evolution*, Spanish edition; book *Dinosaurs of Eden* (children's book for Master Books)

2002 *Did Eve Really Have an Extra Rib?* (book); *Why Won't They Listen?* (book); *101 Signs of Design: Timeless Truths from Genesis;* co-authored book *When Christians Roamed the Earth: Is the Bible-Believing Church Headed for Extinction?* co-authored book *Walking Through Shadows: Finding Hope in a World of Pain; Creation Mini-Series with Ken Ham* (six-part video series, co-produced with Thomas Road Baptist Church, Virginia)

2003 AiG releases *Genesis: The Key to Reclaiming the Culture* (video); *Why Won't They Listen?* (video); *Six Days & the Eisegesis Problem* (video).

2004 In September, the AiG staff of nearly 100 moves from four rented offices in Florence, Kentucky, into one building next to the Creation Museum under construction (Petersburg, Kentucky).

| 2005 | *War of the Worldviews: Powerful Answers for an Evolutionized Culture* (book); *All God's Children: Why We Look Different* (children's book); *Answers Academy* (12-part AiG video series) |

| 2005 | Fundraising for the Creation Museum in full gear — AnswersInGenesis.org receives prestigious Website of the Year award from the National Religious Broadcasters. AiG breaks the $20 million mark in donations for the $27 million Creation Museum and looks forward to a 2007 opening. *Answers* magazine is launched. |

| 2006 | Books include: *The New Answers Book; Genesis of a Legacy* book; *My Creation Bible; It's Designed to Do What It Does Do* |

| 2007 | In January, Answers Worldwide is launched. On May 28, the Creation Museum opens. |

| 2007 | *Darwin's Plantation: Evolution's Racist Roots* (book); *How Could a Loving God?* (book); *Demolishing Strongholds* (12-part AiG video series) |

| 2007 | The ministry begins using its new logo on June 15. |

1:1

answersingenesis

| 2008 | AiG and Ken are presented with the Integrity Award by the National Association of Christian Financial Consultants. AiG records talks in India to be translated into Hindi and Telugu. The petting zoo opens on the Creation Museum's grounds. The Creation Museum's first outdoor live nativity is held in December. |

| 2008 | *The New Answers Book 2; Raising Godly Children in an Ungodly World* (book); *Journey Through the Creation Museum* (book); *The Answers Book for Kids,* Vols. 1 and 2 |

| 2009 | AiG records talks by Ken Ham in Japan. |

| 2009 | *Already Gone* (book); *The Answers Book for Kids,* Vols. 3 and 4; *Dinosaurs for Kids* (book); *The Evolution of Darwin* (three-part AiG video series); *Already Gone: Why Your Kids Will Quit Church and What You Can Do To Stop It* (AiG video); *State of the Nation: The Collapse of Christian America* (AiG video) |

| 2010 | On April 26, the Creation Museum welcomes its one millionth guest (in less than three years). On December 1, AiG's leadership, with Kentucky Governor Steve Beshear and the Ark Encounter LLC of Springfield, Missouri, announced the planned construction of the Ark Encounter in Williamstown, Kentucky. |

| 2010 | Books include: *The New Answers Book 3; One Race, One Blood; Demolishing Supposed Bible Contradictions,* Vol. 1; *State of the Nation: Erosion of Christian America* (AiG video) |

| 2011 | *Answers* magazine is the recipient of the Award of Excellence by the Evangelical Press Association, EPA's top award. In August, 1,000-seat Legacy Hall is opened at the Creation Museum. In November, Ken Ham speaks in front of 1,000 Christian leaders in Malaysia at the All-Asian Creation Conference. In December, the Creation Museum welcomes its 1.5 millionth guest. By the end of the year, translators representing 77 languages had engaged in producing AiG materials. |

2011 Books include: *Already Compromised; How Do We Know the Bible Is True?* Vol. 1; *Begin: A Journey Through Scriptures for Seekers and New Believers; Answers Book for Teens,* Vol. 1; *Demolishing Supposed Bible Contradictions,* Vol. 2; *The Foundations* (six-part AiG video series)

2012 For the second time in six years, AnswersInGenesis.org is the recipient of the Best Ministry Website award from the National Religious Broadcasters. In April, the Johnson Observatory with high-powered telescopes opens on the Creation Museum grounds. *Answers Bible Curriculum* Sunday school program is released.

2012 Books include: *Answers Book for Teens,* Vol. 2; *The True Account of Adam and Eve; How Do We Know the Bible Is True?* Vol. 2

2012 Dedication of the Johnson Observatory at the Creation Museum took place on April 13, 2012.

2012 In October, a revised and expanded edition of *The Lie* is released for the book's 25th anniversary.

Recent picture of the Creation Museum and grounds

INDEX

primeval sea, 47

principles, 5, 14, 17, 29, 57,
66–67, 85–86, 91–94,
102, 109, 137–138, 141,
148, 206, 209

professor, 40, 51, 68, 71, 74,
94, 145, 182, 212

progressive creation, 23, 79,
111, 121, 131, 173, 181,
204, 209

prophecy, 11, 75, 185, 187,
189, 191

public school, 37, 44, 65, 67,
70–71, 85, 120, 135, 164,
175–176, 200, 216

races, 59–61, 142–145, 194,
220

racism, 41, 60–61, 142,
144–145, 217, 226

radio, 25, 36, 51, 177, 180,
221, 225

rebellion, 55, 69, 107, 110,
113–116, 157, 188, 190,
207

redemption, 39, 135, 158, 167,
171, 211

relative morality, 34, 88, 157

religion, 9, 14, 28, 30–31, 35,
40, 43–46, 48, 51–53, 62,
69–72, 89, 95, 99, 108,
157, 164, 174, 177–178,
205, 225

Resurrection, 24, 56, 107, 116,
133, 140, 158–159, 162,
167, 202

revival, 19, 170–171

rib, 99, 115, 178–179, 226

rocks, 45–46, 146, 189

role reversal, 102

sacrifice, 55, 103–104, 116,
123, 161

salvation, 56, 74–75, 121, 123,
163, 169, 177, 191, 195,
204, 211

Satan, 23–24, 82, 167, 207

savages, 112, 143

scholars, 19, 95, 122, 132, 183,
209, 216

science, 7, 9, 11, 18, 31,
35–36, 40–41, 45–47,
49–52, 57–68, 70, 72–74,
76, 126, 130–131, 144,
156–157, 164, 166, 169,
173, 177–178, 182, 189,
200, 203, 207, 212,
215–216, 218, 221–224

Scopes Trial, 60, 225

seminaries, 14, 88, 210

serpent, 23–24, 140, 148, 202

shepherds, 11, 173, 178, 180,
184

sin, 17, 39, 53, 55–56, 69,
76, 82–83, 101, 103–105,
107, 109–111, 113–120,
122–125, 127, 129, 135,
139, 157–160, 162,
186–188, 195, 204–206,
208, 210

sinful, 109–110, 114, 116,
128, 188, 190

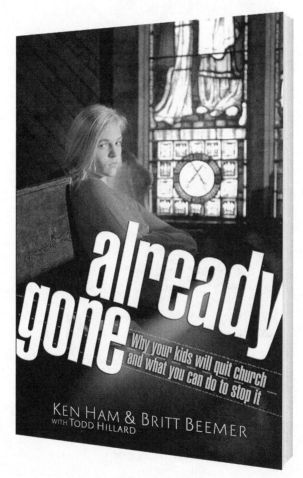

Get Connected!
answersingenesis.org

Website
- Latest biblical and scientific answers
- Free online videos and books
- Upcoming events and blogs
- More great books, DVDs, and curricula

Free Mobile App
- Quick biblical and scientific answers
- Digital videos and books
- Digital witnessing tool
- Latest articles, blogs, and more

App available November 2012

answersingenesis.org

The Lie
PHOTO CONTEST!

A prize a week for 25 weeks!

Grab your camera and get creative! Win **up to $500 in prizes** by showing your new copy of *The Lie* in a special way. In celebration of the 25th anniversary of this top-selling book and the release of the revised, updated and expanded edition, a prize a week for 25 weeks will be awarded! It culminates with the Grand Prize award in May, 2013.

For complete details and contest guidelines, go to **facebook.com/creationmuseum.**